LIFE AT THE LIMITS

Olympic Peninsula, Washington

LIFE AT THE LIMITS

Photographs and Text
by
WALTER KAUFMANN

Olympic Peninsula, Washington

READER'S DIGEST PRESS
Distributed
by
McGraw-Hill, Inc.
NEW YORK
1978

Life at the Limits

Drab is the sun's endless motion
compared to the burst
of life when it slakes
its fiery thirst
in the sea and drowns. And the ocean
is most beautiful where it breaks.

ACKNOWLEDGEMENTS

My wife, Hazel, accompanied me on the long trips on which most of the photographs were taken. Taking the pictures, I usually walked alone; but it made a difference to know that I was not totally alone.

Moshe Barasch called my attention to some very interesting books and articles.

Getting a work with so many color photographs published required a long uphill fight. Nicolas Ducrot bore the brunt of it, gave me unswerving support, and prevailed.

In the fall of 1977, Jill Anderson helped me to improve the text. Her total reliability and exceptional sensitivity made it delightful to work with her.

Jo Kaufmann did a splendid job copyediting the text and made many helpful suggestions.

Library of Congress Cataloging in Publication Data

Kaufmann, Walter Arnold.
   Life at the limits.

   Bibliography: p.
   1. Life in art. 2. Arts. 3. Life. I. Title.
NX650.L54K38   700   78-9506
ISBN 0-07-033315-7

This book was originated and produced by
VISUAL BOOKS, INC.
342 Madison Avenue
New York, New York 10017

Ein Grabmal für

BRUNO KAUFMANN
1881–1956
EDITH KAUFMANN
1887–1977

Olympic Peninsula, Washington

CONTENTS

NOTES ON THE PHOTOGRAPHS

NOTES ON THE PHOTOGRAPHS

The black and white photographs have captions.

The first ten color photographs and the last two were taken in Khajuraho, all the rest in Benares and Calcutta.

The last eleven color pages of Benares show scenes along the river Ganges, including three photographs on facing pages of the two burning ghats where people who have died in the city are cremated. The photographs of Calcutta begin with the picture of a book stall.

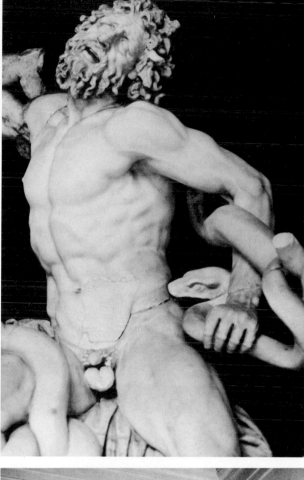

TOP LEFT: Queen Tiye, ca. 1370 B.C. Wood (9.4 cm)
Ägyptisches Museum, Berlin-West. Foto: Jürgen Liepe.
TOP RIGHT: Laokoon, detail, 1st century B.C. (2.42 m)
Vatican Museum.

LEFT: Etruscan She-Wolf, 5th century B.C. Bronze. (85 cm)
Capitoline Museum, Rome.
RIGHT: Gigantic head of the Emperor Constantine, 4th century A.D. Bronze.
Palazzo dei Conservatori, Rome. The Leica case gives some idea of the size.

Dying Persian, Hellenistic, 3rd century B.C. Terme Museum, Rome. Life size marble. Usually shown only in reclining position, but changing the angle changes the expression. BELOW: Ancient Roman heads. Villa Giulia, Rome

Etruscan sarcophagus, late 6th century B.C. Villa Giulia, Rome
Etruscan sarcophagi, 2nd-1st century B.C. Museum, Volterra

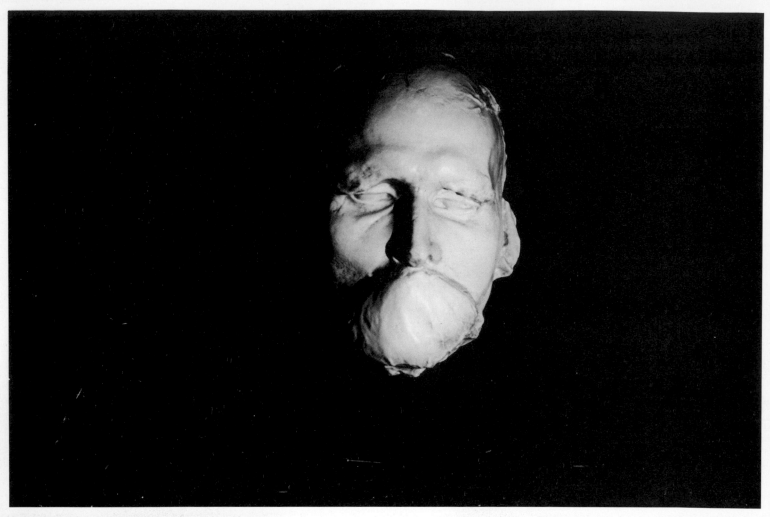

Nietzsche's Death Mask. Nietzsche Haus, Sils Maria, Switzerland. LEFT: Roman sphinx, 2nd or 1st century B.C., Palazzo dei Conservatori, Rome. RIGHT: Etruscan sarcophagus, 2nd-1st century B.C., Museum in Volterra, Italy.

Capuchin catacombs, Palermo

Capuchin "cemetery," Via Veneto, Rome

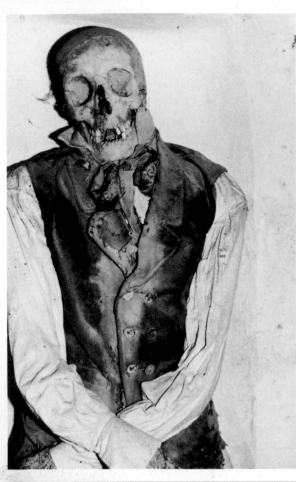

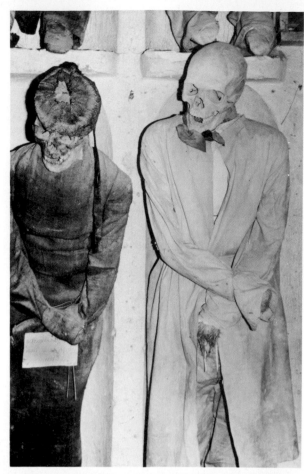

Capuchin catacombs,
Palermo.

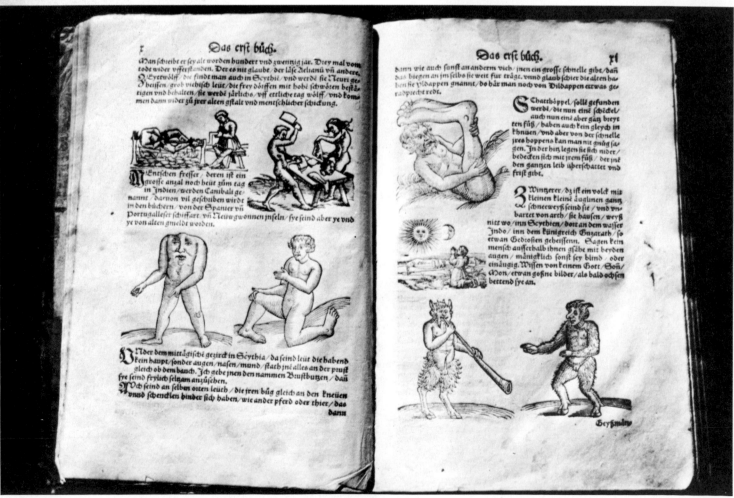

Wunderwerck, Basel 1557; that is: "Wondrous Works or God's Unfathomable Modeling . . .
all ornamented with beautiful illustrations . . ."

TOP LEFT: Rembrandt (1606–1669): Self-portrait of 1661, detail. Rijksmuseum, Amsterdam. TOP RIGHT: Michelangelo (1475–1564): Night (about 1530). Medici Chapel, Florence. LEFT: Michelangelo: The Pieta of Palestrina (after 1552). Academy, Florence. According to De Tolnay, vol. V, pp. 152ff., by a follower of Michelangelo: RIGHT: Michelangelo: Boboli Slave. Academy. Florence, 1530–34, according to De Tolnay, vol. V, p. 60.

Sanchi, India: transistor radio above the Buddha.
Sanchi, India: playing cards in the shade.

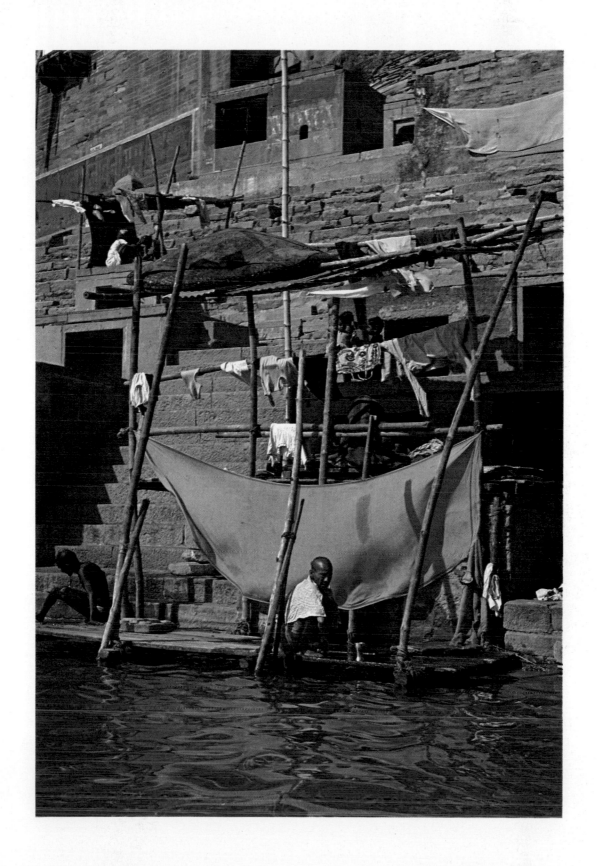

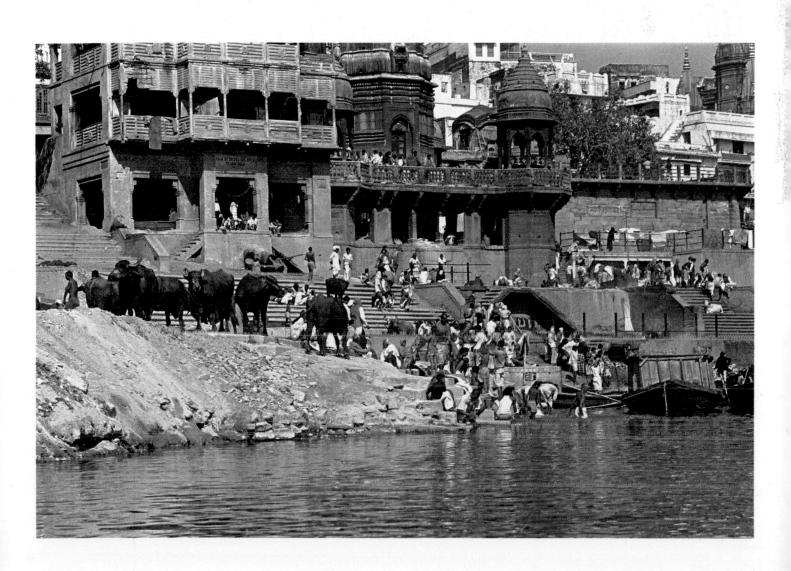

PROLOGUE

1

Most philosophy has no sense for art and is much the worse for that. What major philosopher since Plato could one possibly call "an artistic Socrates," except Nietzsche, who coined this beautiful image? And even Plato and Nietzsche had little feeling for the visual arts.

The point is not that art is so important that philosophers should not ignore it. A few of them have, after all, dealt with aesthetics, even if they showed in the process, as Kant did, that they lacked a sense for art. What makes not only much work on aesthetics but most philosophy so academic is not the common failure to understand what art *is* but the refusal to see what art *shows*.

Much of the greatest art shows us life at the limits, which almost all philosophers have ignored. Existentialism poses as the one great exception and bases its claim for wide attention on its exploration of extreme situations. Indeed, the most important feature that the so-called existentialists have in common is the belief that our most extreme experiences furnish the proper starting point for philosophy. In some areas of philosophy it actually makes much better sense to start with very different problems; but if one seeks some insight into the human condition, one cannot afford to ignore life at the limits, and I believe that reflection on this subject is the best way to begin a trilogy on man's lot.

Most existentialist studies of extreme situations are disappointing. The German existentialists in particular have worked with a conception of life at the limits that suggests a grotesquely narrow range of experience and of acquaintance with the arts. Kierkegaard did add to our understanding of dread and despair, which he knew intimately, and in *The Sickness unto Death* he distinguished the flavors of different kinds of despair with the expertise of a wine taster. His successors have never advanced very far beyond the two moods he discussed, and now it is widely assumed that life at the limits means dread and despair.

A quick way of sketching a more inclusive and differentiated conception of life at the limits is to present two lists, A and B. Each involves a progression, but not a necessary sequence in which every stage entails the next. The first table lists some conditions that come to us, as it were from outside; but on reflection we see that all but the first of these (in one of its two senses) can be invited or chosen. The second table lists human responses, but again the line between what befalls us and what we choose is not always easy to draw.

A

1. *delivery (birth and giving birth)*
2. *deformity*
3. *disaster*
4. *defeat*
5. *disgrace*
6. *destitution (including extreme hunger and thirst)*
7. *distress*
8. *desolation and darkness (including deafness and blindness)*
9. *dehumanization*
10. *danger*
11. *decay*
12. *death*

B

1. *dread*
2. *depth (intensity and profundity)*
3. *disillusionment*
4. *despair, depression, despondence, dejection*
5. *derangement, delusions, dreams, drunkenness, drugs*
6. *debauchery, dissipation, dissoluteness*
7. *degradation of others*
8. *destruction (including suicide and murder)*
9. *defiance*
10. *devotion, love*
11. *Dionysian joy (often associated with music)*
12. *Dionysian abandon (often associated with dance)*

Looking at the first table, one may feel at first glance that these states are, after all, dismal and that one might just as well lump them together as suffering. Yet disaster and destitution, dehumanization and danger, decay and death need not be experienced as suffering. And those not inclined to reflect on such states can learn this from art.

The approach adopted in this book is as unusual as its subject matter. We shall try to gain some understanding of life at the limits through a series of ninety-four color photographs, as well as reflections on a number of poems and works of art. This may be more fruitful than prolonged analyses of these twenty-four categories. Still, a few comments on these tables are called for.

Why is disease not included? Because it confronts us with the limits either as a disaster that strikes suddenly or as distress, danger, or decay. Often it takes several or even all of these forms.

Destitution may seem to be merely one form of distress. But the color photographs show how destitution is by no means always a form of distress. The destitute may be cheerful as well as beautiful, and destitution may also be chosen deliberately, not as a form of suffering.

Danger may be exhilarating and actively sought. Nor was it merely perverse of Baudelaire when he celebrated "the gorgeous iridescence of decay." Death is not always painful either, nor do all people dread it. Poets and artists can teach us all this and much more; also, for example, that those who shut their eyes to life at the limits lead an impoverished existence.

The last two categories may call for some comment. Mere pleasure and delight are usually not extreme states; but Dionysian joy, which affirms the world, in spite of its terrors, takes us to the limits, and none of the other arts can express and evoke it as well as music.

Dionysian abandon should be distinguished from Dionysian joy and from the "abandonment" of existentialism (*délaissement*). The existentialists have stressed forsakenness and desolation. Dionysian abandon however, is typically not solitary, and it is not necessarily joyous. It was probably experienced by many participants in the ancient festivals of Dionysus, and Euripides has given us a blood-curdling account of it in his *Bacchae*. An excellent anthropological description is included in *The Interpretation of Cultures: Selected Essays* by Clifford Geertz (1973). Chapter 4, "Religion as a Cultural System," contains five pages (114–18) on the Balinese Barong dance:

> By the time a full-scale Rangda-Barong encounter has been concluded, a majority, often nearly all, of the members of the group sponsoring it will have become caught up in it not just imaginatively but bodily. . . . Usually sheer pandemonium breaks out at this point with members of the crowd, of both sexes, falling into trance all around the courtyard and rushing out to stab themselves, wrestle with one another, devour live chicks or excrement. . . .

As long as one merely talks about twenty-four terms, the discussion is almost bound to be scholastic. The words take on flesh not only in the photographs but also in some of the poems, paintings, and sculptures that will be discussed. The works of some outstanding artists and writers show how differentiated their experiences were. These people were far indeed from simply responding to death with dread, and to distress with despair. Life at the limits is infinitely richer than that.

It remains odd that in English all twenty-four terms begin with a "d." That feat would be hard, if not impossible, to duplicate in another language. In English, however, the words chosen here seem to be the best there are. There are only a few cases in which this might well be questioned. "Birth" may seem preferable to "delivery," but the latter term has the advantage of also referring to the mother's experience, which certainly should not be ignored. "Poverty" is a term used more often than "destitution" but is really not what is meant and would need to be qualified by "extreme." "Depth" has the virtue of covering both intensity and profundity, and it also suggests that by attaining sufficient depth one approaches the limits.

Is it a mere accident that all these words begin with the same letter? Most of them actually begin with the same two letters (de), but many of these are not derived from the Latin prefix *de*, which signifies separation and usually also a descent, a downward motion. It will be noted that "down" and "deep" also begin with a "d"—like danger, death, and dread. But that there are so many terms with the same first letter is clearly due to the Latin prefixes. *Dis* in Latin also suggests separation, and we may conclude that most often it is a separation from a sheltered state that brings a confrontation with the limits. Conversely, this departure may be actively sought in a quest for the boundaries.

A scholastic philosopher might give marks to artists and writers for each of the categories they explored, or classify them, or construct neat conceptual schemes. If each of the twelve experiences in the first table could be met with each of the twelve responses in the second, that alone would yield 144 possibilities. An academician could double the number by distinguishing cases in which one confronts one's own deformity and that of others, and so forth down the list. Even death and delivery need not stop him, for one can confront one's own death and then not die immediately; and delivery has been defined to include the mother's experience. Nor need those who thrive on quantity stop with 288. Each of the twelve conditions can be met with a complex response that combines any number of items from list B. Moreover, one might also be struck by more than one item from list A. And such a combination of conditions could also be met by one or more responses from the second list. There is work here even for those who like to use computers.

The main reason for offering the two tables at the outset is to save the phrase "life at the limits" from being mere words and to show at a glance what is at stake. Life at the limits can be, though it is by no means always felt to be, exhilarating.

My ultimate purpose is to gain a better understanding of the human condition. That is a major undertaking, and this volume is the first part of a trilogy to which *Religions in Four*

Dimensions could be considered an overture. The second part is *Time Is an Artist,* and the last *What Is Man?* Both volumes include a series of color photographs, as well as black-and-white pictures, and the range of the pictures is far wider than in the present book. All these volumes abandon traditional forms. They are bold adventures in line with Nietzsche's well-grounded faith that "the secret for harvesting from existence the greatest fruitfulness and the greatest enjoyment is—to *live dangerously.*"

The photographs in the last volume show people of many lands. Those in the second concentrate on time's artistry in nature and time's work on art, including bronze and stone, ruins and so-called restorations. The text of *Time Is an Artist* deals also with human attitudes toward time and change, youth and age, the old and the new. The theme of temporality and its importance for understanding human existence has been sounded by some of the existentialists, but again my approach and results could scarcely be more different.

The color photographs in this book are not meant to illustrate the twenty-four categories. They are not conceived as illustrations or a survey of any kind. So far from being subservient to philosophy, they concentrate on aspects of life at the limits and on human responses that are not dreamt of in traditional philosophy. The text provides a larger setting and explores this theme in many perspectives. The color photographs are not discussed before the Epilogue, but the chapters could be seen as a spiral path that gradually comes closer and closer to the color pictures. Unlike the pictures, the text may seem in one or two places to approximate a survey, but on reflection this appearance will be found to be misleading. The aim is to provide a text that is in its own way as rich as the photographs and not exhausted by a single reading. For a start, one might note that they show how beautiful the people in one village and two cities are. Perhaps also that they do not show delivery, deformity, and disaster but explore one kind of life at the limits in depth.

I

MUSIC AND NATURE

2

Much of the greatest art is terror transfigured, a celebration of life at the limits. Tragedy is the clearest example. But some great artists have followed a different path; for example, Giotto, Fra Angelico, and Botticelli. And at first glance, music may seem to be closer to them than to tragedy. Yet one kind of music closely resembles tragedy: opera. And in *Boris Godunov*, the most famous Russian opera, the terror is overwhelming.

German, Italian, and French operas differ widely, but almost all of the best loved transfigure stories that in real life would have been thought to be very depressing. Violetta dies of consumption; Aida and Radames are buried alive; Rigoletto carries a corpse in a sack and discovers that it is his daughter's—all in Verdi. Puccini tries to make torture, consumption, and heartbreak beautiful; Donizetti madness. In *Carmen*, by far the most widely admired French opera, we see betrayal, despair, and murder. Wagner rather consistently deals with extreme states, and the most popular music he ever wrote is probably Isolde's *Liebestod*. Richard Strauss seems to have been determined to bring on the stage in his *Salomé* horrors surpassing those in all previous operas.

People pay a great deal of money to see these operas, and in retrospect they often count such occasions among the high points of their existence. Clearly, the pleasure such music gives is not sadistic, and what the audience is seeking is not cheap thrills. What is sought, also when one listens to music like this at home, is liberation from the mainstream of life. What is wanted is a confrontation with the limits.

Some of the finest operas are rather different from those mentioned or alluded to so far. Beethoven's *Fidelio* ends joyously. Yet this was the first opera performed in Salzburg after the end of World War II and the discovery of the death camps, and the scene in which the political prisoners circle the stage was almost unbearable. When the opera was performed in Salzburg on a much larger stage in 1968, right after the Soviet invasion of Czechoslovakia, the experience was no less harrowing. After all, the scene throughout is a political prison, and its anguish pervades the entire opera. What makes the joy of the finale Dionysian, both in *Fidelio* and in Beethoven's *Ninth Symphony*, is that the composer did not avert his eyes from terror.

Opera and the *Ninth Symphony* are, of course, special cases. Most music may seem to be very different. Yet Gustav Mahler's, for example, really is not that different. His "Songs on the Death of Children" furnish a striking example, and his symphonies also are scarcely endurable.

Still, not all music is like that. Mozart and Haydn, Handel and Bach seem to dwell in another world, and there is no music I love more than theirs and Beethoven's late quartets. And what of Gluck, Monteverdi, and other early composers? Some of the greatest works of these men deal clearly with life at the limits: Mozart's *Requiem* and *Don Giovanni*, Bach's *St. John Passion* and *St. Matthew Passion*, Haydn's *Mass in Time of War*, Gluck's and Monteverdi's versions of the Orpheus story, and Handel's *Hallelujah Chorus*. There is a multitude of ways of experiencing life at the limits, and lovers of music will be able to think of scores of examples not mentioned here. I am doing little more than pointing to a few that may help to show how superficial two widespread notions are; namely, that life at the limits is simply unpleasant, and that one responds to it with either dread or despair. There may be components of dread and despair in the composer's experience and in our response to it, but despair is not always the end of delight.

It does not require a morbid mind like Kierkegaard's to savor some kind of despair. People unable to do that are shut off from much of the world's greatest art. But it is doubtful that anyone really lacks this capacity. It is only by sticking to words, words, words that one is led to suppose that despair must preclude delight.

Pure music may still seem to be a world apart from operas and songs, masses and passions. Does it have any bearing on life at the limits? Much of it does in an obvious way. It can achieve an intensity rarely, if ever, found in the other arts. To that end it does not require words or a stage. One may think of music as the language of the emotions, provided one adds that the terms we have to name emotions are grotesquely few and inadequate—like the names we have for colors—and music does not so much illustrate or lend a voice to emotions that one could name, such as envy, jealousy, anger, as it gives expression to what had seemed inexpressible.

Serious artists are people who refuse to remain silent about things of which they cannot speak—in ordinary language. That is also true of poets. And philosophy also can be, but rarely is, an attempt to show what transcends ordinary discourse. Some philosophers, notably including some existentialists, have assumed that this requires an outrageous jargon that abounds in ugly coinages.

Pure music takes another path. We close our eyes as we listen to it and enter a realm beyond sight and touch, a world one cannot explore by walking, swimming, or flying, a second nature with laws of its own, and heights and abysses, measurements, feelings, terror, and beauty. Music is a triumphant rejection of the world into which we are born, a "No" to nature, a bold defiance of God and gods and whatever nonhuman powers are thought to have fashioned the cosmos; it is a rival world made by man.

Pure music is not so much life at the limits as life beyond them. That is why critics have sometimes used words like "ethereal," "heavenly," and "otherworldly" to describe it. But such words have a misleading religious ring.

I am far from believing that all music was born of despair or that all music brings to mind life at the limits. Some of the most beautiful music by Haydn, for example, does not. But Beethoven's indomitable strength and Mozart's gaiety keep opening up to us the infinite variety of life at the limits, which need not be dreary or melodramatic. It is tempting to say that no response could be nobler or more beautiful than *Eine kleine Nachtmusik*. But in literature and art we shall discover very different responses, and it would be silly to attempt to rank them. What matters is to leave behind our preconceptions about the limits and to realize how differently sensitive people have experienced them.

To that end these extremely brief reflections on the world of music may suffice. They are little more than reminders of familiar compositions that cannot be reproduced here but should be seen in a new perspective if we want to understand human existence. Literature, philosophy, and the visual arts will be considered at greater length. And short poems have the advantage that a few can be reproduced here and reread again and again. In these areas I have done some previous work in formats that allowed for some scholarly apparatus, and to avoid superficiality it may help if now and then I can refer skeptics to more detailed studies that support my argument. Hence I shall occasionally refer to some of my own writings in which relevant materials and rival interpretations are discussed more fully.

3

The beauties of nature and those of art are worlds apart. Hence some philosophers have actually questioned whether it makes any sense to call anything natural beautiful. But it is perverse to define beauty in such a way that only art is beautiful. Some philosophers generate problems and paradoxes simply by redefining terms in odd ways.

It is from nature that we derive our notions of beauty. As children we learn the meaning of "beautiful" not from music, poems, or sculptures but from flowers, butterflies, and "beautiful" mornings; perhaps also "beautiful" faces.

Landscapes and seascapes furnish the paradigms of the sublime. Music and poetry are sublime when they reach vaguely comparable heights. And the sublime is always close to terror. To be awe-inspiring is part of its meaning. But beauty does not have to be of that kind. Flowers and butterflies are not terrifying. They are quite unlike the rocky crags of the Dolomites or the sea in a hurricane. Much of nature's beauty is clearly remote from life at the limits.

Yet nothing large in nature is more widely acclaimed as beautiful than many sunsets. No tragic sense of life is required, no morbid taste; at this point those who admire the boldest paintings of Turner and those who love *kitsch* agree, though what they experience is clearly different. Sunrise is equally to the point and no less evocative of life at the limits, even as birth is no less an extreme situation than death.

Few if any landscapes are more moving than those suggesting life at the limits: the sea in a storm, surf pounding rocks, mountains, desert, the outback, the renewal of life in the spring, and the colors of fall. But to supplement the black-and-white photographs and the poem in the opening pages of this volume, it may suffice to quote three short poems from my *Cain and Other Poems*. The first, "Autumn," was prompted by Giuseppe di Lampedusa's *The Leopard*. The author had never published anything, but in his old age, during his last year, he wrote this beautiful novel and died.

Autumn

Hard is the maple's wood,
unbending the trunk, almost grey,
buried in darkness the roots,
a tree among trees in May.

Touched by the autumn frost
when the birds no longer sing,
the leaves about to be lost
outdazzle the plumage of spring.

Even the sunlight was dull
till it struck their weightless form:
what matter that soon they fall,
carried away in a storm?

From
The Burning Bush

Summers one sees and can count,
and the frost
one expects
like night.

Winter once awaits
like white thunder,

but the splendor
of fall

is lightning
piercing the peace
of hearts
ready for darkness.

Foliage

November
like night
makes my window
a mirror.

Golden fire
burns itself out
against a dark sky
with no future
to dim its brightness.

Why fade into winter?
Why mourn the azaleas?
Masses of leaves on the ground
do not dull the flaming foliage
but make the earth glow.

Leafless
the elm imprints
grace to the last
on the iron sky.

II

WESTERN LITERATURE

4

What are the most renowned works of English literature? *Lear* and *Hamlet*, plays in which the deaths are hard to keep track of and the hero's despair reaches depths not charted since Euripides and Sophocles died in 406 B.C. And next to *Hamlet* and *Lear*, *Macbeth* and *Othello*. They are almost equally grim and inspired two of Verdi's great operas. And next to them some of Shakespeare's other tragedies and his black comedies.

Almost nothing in Western literature is in the same league, except the most stupendous Greek tragedies. They, too, portray life at the limits: Prometheus crucified, Agamemnon murdered by his wife, Clytemnestra by her son. Greek poetry reached its greatest heights in transfiguring tales like these. Suffering that seemed to defy endurance was brought on the stage and made beautiful by stunning language and new perspectives.

That was the very essence of tragedy and the supreme achievement of Greek literature. The plays that are judged the most beautiful surpass all the rest in terror. If any tragedy has been admired even more than *Lear* and *Hamlet*, *Prometheus* and the *Oresteia*, it is surely *Antigone* or *Oedipus Tyrannus*. Both are so packed with horror that only a supreme poet could have made tales like these beautiful.

The stuff of tragedy is suffering transcending the worst we have known, suffering we cannot cope with—but the poet can, and he makes us see it as beautiful, although he is not sadistic. He does not reduce those who suffer to objects that we might view as tools of our pleasure. He leads us to look up to them as superior. We do not pity them; we are awed by their stature, share their suffering, and find comfort in their ability to endure what we could not.

In comedy, not in tragedy, there is a sadistic element. The plot can be the same, but instead of sharing the suffering we are invited to laugh at it. Yet no pure comedy has ever attained the rank of the greatest tragedies. The only comedies that the best judges consider almost as beautiful as the best tragedies are a few tragicomedies or black comedies born of the most profound despair, like *The Merchant of Venice*, *Measure for Measure*, and *The Tempest*. Let those who can, laugh at Shylock and Caliban!

If there is one work of Greek literature that is in no way inferior to the major Greek tragedies, it is the *Iliad*, the epic that deals with Achilles' madness and records in gory detail the deaths of countless heroes. The landscape of the *Iliad* smells of death which is ever-present, and yet the poem is not depressing because it is vibrant with fierce vitality. It is an epic of war but not realistic, tawdry, or seamy. It is a triumph of style, imagination, and beauty. Greek tragedy derived its inspiration from this epic, and all Western tragedies are based on Greek tragedy.

The *Iliad* is also the mother of Western epic poetry. Tradition has it that the *Odyssey* was composed later by the same poet, because it is in many ways similar. Yet the sensibility of the *Odyssey* would seem to belong to a somewhat later age. The central theme: heartbreak, death upon death, and in the end a terrible slaughter. But from the grounds of despair the poet reaps a magnificent harvest, not a mere tale of daring adventures and bare survival but a poem that, like the *Iliad*, has given delight to untold generations.

No Western epic has ever equaled these two. The few that have entered the contest have also tried to transfigure terror. Vergil's *Aeneid* is closely modeled on Homer's *Odyssey* and was an attempt to do for the Romans what he had done for the Greeks. Dante's *Divine Comedy* enters the lists by employing Vergil as Dante's guide to the underworld, first explored by Homer's Odysseus and then by Vergil's Aeneas. Dante's underworld is far more terrible: not the classical world of shadows but the hell of Christianity. Dante pushes beyond the limits of life to explore life after death and devotes the first and most celebrated of the three parts of his epic to the *Inferno*, dealing with unbearable suffering endured in eternity. This is accounted the greatest triumph of Christian literature.

5

Later epics do not compare with the works of Homer, Vergil, and Dante. But the modern world produced a new kind of epic, dispensing with verse: the novel. This is incomparably easier to handle, and there are more mediocre examples than any one person could list. But most of the greatest novels explore life at the limits.

The first major German novel, *Simplicissimus*, written in the seventeenth century, deals with the horrors of the Thirty Years' War as experienced by a simpleton. Almost precisely a hundred years later, Goethe's first novel, *The Sufferings of the Young Werther*, dealt with the hero's mounting despair and eventual suicide. It became an instant best seller all over Europe and inspired a wave of suicides.

No French novel is more famous than Victor Hugo's *Notre Dame de Paris*, whose hero is a hunchback, unless it is the same author's *Les Misérables*. But no novel written in Western Europe can brook comparison with the masterpieces of Dostoevsky and Tolstoy, whose international impact brings to mind Shakespeare, Greek tragedy, and Homer.

The plots of Dostoevsky's most influential novels revolve around epilepsy, derangement, murder, and miscarried justice. He explores madness, feelings of guilt and consuming resentment, and utter despair. But instead of piling horror on horror, he shows us all kinds of misery in new and unexpected perspectives, adding to our understanding of the human condition.

Tolstoy's temperament was very different. Instead of compelling the reader to dwell in the soul of murderers and madmen, he often seems to look down on our follies from Mount Olympus. Yet he tips his hand in the opening sentence of *Anna Karenina*: "Happy families are all alike; every unhappy family is unhappy in its own way." This is his way of saying that happiness is rather dull and not worth writing about, while misery is the substance of literature. And when too many readers missed his central concern with life at the limits, he decided to become painfully explicit and wrote *The Death of Ivan Ilyitch*, a tale about a man dying in pain.

If anyone after Tolstoy and Dostoevsky has written novels that can be compared to theirs, it is Solzhenitsyn. In Chapter 34 of his *Cancer Ward* a scrubwoman in the ward says to one of the patients:

> School children write compositions: On the Unhappy, Tragic . . . Life of Anna Karenina. But was Anna really unhappy? She chose passion—and paid for passion, that's happiness! She was free and proud! But what if, in peacetime, men in caps and overcoats come into the house where you were born, where you've lived all your life, and order the whole family to leave the house and the city in twenty-four hours, taking only what your weak hands can carry? . . . and your little daughter in a hair-ribbon sits down to play Mozart for the last time, but bursts out crying and runs away,—why should I re-read *Anna Karenina*? Maybe I've suffered enough? Where can I read about *us, about us*?
> And although she had almost begun to shout, still her training by many years of terror did not desert her: she was not shouting; it was not a real shout. Indeed, it was only Kostoglotov who heard her.*

Perhaps someone said something rather like this to Solzhenitsyn when he was a patient in a cancer ward. In any case, he decided to write about men and women whose sufferings had remained mute, though perhaps they dwarfed the tribulations of most of the heroes of literature. Solzhenitsyn's works deal with life under Stalin's tyranny, above all with the torments in the camps and a cancer ward.

At first glance, he may seem to have turned against the Western literary tradition. Formerly, it is widely thought, there was always a hero whom fate exalted even as it destroyed him. His very destruction was glorious. There is some truth in that, but this widespread conception is still misleading.

Greek tragedy was more than fifty years old and Aeschylus, its creator, had been dead twenty-five when Euripides wrote the first tragedy that clearly had one tragic hero—or rather a heroine: Medea, who killed her own children. Not only had the focus shifted in Aeschylus' trilogies, and the separate plays were not meant to be self-contained, but in *Agamemnon* and in *The Eumenides* there was no one hero, and in *The Suppliants* and, still more clearly so, in *The Persians* the sufferers were many. This had also been true of the *Iliad*. Sophocles soon adopted Euripides' great

* Kathryn Feuer's translation. See Bibliography.

innovation in some of *his* plays, most notably in his *Oedipus Tyrannus*, and eventually many critics and readers came to believe that in tragedy there is always, perhaps even by definition, a tragic hero. But in some of the later tragedies of both Sophocles and Euripides there is not. And even in those that do have one hero, like *Oedipus Tyrannus*, those who suffer and are destroyed are often many. That is also true of *Hamlet* and *Lear*, and in some of Shakespeare's most famous tragedies there is more than one hero: *Romeo and Juliet, Antony and Cleopatra*, and perhaps also *Julius Caesar*. Even when there are two, of course, both may be raised to a higher stature. The question remains whether that is actually what happens. In Aeschylus' *Persians* and Euripides' *Trojan Women*, to give only two examples, large numbers of people are destroyed wantonly without much glory. And this is also obvious in *Lear* and *Hamlet*. Ophelia has many sisters.

Conversely, Solzhenitsyn's novels do not lack heroes. Though he refrains from placing one over-life-size man at the center, there is one person in each of the novels who clearly resembles the author more than anyone else does, and he is a hero—but not the only one. Quite as much as the tragic poets before him, the author celebrates courage and defiance—also honesty—and he allows his heroes to triumph by absolutely refusing to yield their integrity. The author's moral intensity is as plain as Tolstoy's was or Dostoevsky's. It is free of self-righteousness and balanced throughout by savage wit. Rarely has sarcasm scaled such heights.

As we survey Western literature from the *Iliad* to Solzhenitsyn's war novel, *August 1914*, we find an impressive unity in the most celebrated tragedies, epics, and novels. They do not merely eschew happy families or include some unpleasantness. They plumb the ultimate depths of human despair and suffering without ever seeking to plunge the reader into a state of hopelessness. In one way or another they always transfigure terror.

Of course, there are Western plays, novels, and even epics that are less grim, and many are quite amusing. It remains worthy of note that the plays, novels, and epics that are widely considered the greatest deal relentlessly with life at the limits. The greatest comedies do this also but seek relief not in tears but in laughter. And works whose subject matter is really light are judged to be mere *divertimenti*.

The point is not to impose my value judgments. Far from it. I would gladly trade most non-Greek and non-Shakespearean tragedies for the *divertimenti* of Mozart. But Mozart's *divertimenti* are not the works of a man who stops short of the limits, averting his eyes. They are the gifts of one who has crossed the limits.

6

One form of great literature may seem to be an exception: short poems. Partly on that account they seem to have lost their hold on the imagination of those who have grown up since World War II. Poems that nourished the souls of earlier generations, lines that one learned by heart as one came to feel that one had a soul, now seem irrelevant. Unlike the *Iliad*, *Oedipus*, or *The Trojan Women*, odes to flowers and birds no longer matter.

In "A Journal in Verse," written in 1961 and included in my *Cain*, the poem preceding "The Eichmann Trial" is:

Romanticism

I heard an old harlot sighing:
Look at the green trees and the dew!
I heard a young whore replying:
What are the green trees to you?

I can see how a poet thrills
to the arias of nightingales
and to valleys of daffodils;
but when he faints and fails

or, worse, has intimations
and fills with ecstasy
pages of ostentations,
what is all that to me?

I doubt that a human heart
could ever have felt half the rapture
that reams of romantic art
never entirely capture.

I heard a young whore sighing:
Some of them felt all they said.
I heard an old harlot replying:
They strain, but their hearts are dead.

Short poems do not survive translation as well as novels, epics, and plays. The inadequacy of English translations of Russian novels has often been noted but has not kept them from having an overwhelming impact on countless readers and writers, including critics and poets. No English version of Homer comes close to the beauty of the original, but even the prose translation by E.V. Rieu communicates the *Iliad's* poetic grandeur. To render Greek tragedy into English is even harder, and still the vision and the power survive somehow, even as Mozart survives in indifferent performances. In the same way, Shakespeare has left his mark on world literature, although no translation can equal his matchless poetry. Much is lost, but in all these cases enough gets across not only to make a profound impression but to change the sensibility even of foreign readers.

Short poems are not so fortunate. They have no overpowering plots or unforgettable characters; they cannot uncover layers of self-deception as they probe the depths of the human soul; they cannot create a whole society and let us breathe an atmosphere altogether different from all we are used to. They are too short for all that and rely on little but language, often on what is peculiar to one tongue, on words that happen to rhyme, on similar sounds, on meters, on music begotten by nothing but words. Hence it is harder for poems of this kind to become part of world literature or at least part of the West's common heritage.

Nevertheless, those to whom literature means a great deal agree in esteeming many short poems as some of the greatest creations of humanity. And is there not room in this format for the beauty of flowers and butterflies? Of course, there is, even as there is room for amusing novels and plays. There are many mansions in art, and it would be folly to try to force its variety into a single mold.

Portentousness is a fault, and wit is a touch of grace even in tragedy, epic, and novel. Light verse is a wonderful genre and can have depth. But it is striking that all the major poets who wrote short poems have dealt again and again with life at the limits.

7

Shakespeare's sonnets are the most obvious case in point. This most impressive sequence of short poems by any poet in any language revolves around death, decay, and despair. One of his younger contemporaries also wrote a cycle of sonnets: John Donne. None of these has won greater fame than "Death, be not proud . . ." The outstanding English poet of the later seventeenth century was John Milton, who surpassed himself in his sonnet "On His Blindness."

Even Shakespeare's sonnets often do not end as strongly as they begin. Perhaps another of Milton's sonnets has the most powerful last line of any English short poem. It also deals with the poet's blindness and begins:

Methought I saw my late espoused Saint
Brought to me like *Alcestis* from the grave . . .

It ends:

I wak'd, she fled, and day brought back my night.

Of Milton's not quite so short poems none has been anthologized more often than "Lycidas," an elegy on a friend who was drowned. After that, the best-known English poem before the beginning of the romantic movement is probably Thomas Gray's "Elegy Written in a Country Churchyard."

The romantics, too, did not by any means write only about birds and flowers. Robert Burns wrote two famous poems, "To a Mouse" and "To a Louse." More to the point, Byron devoted a superb short poem to "The Destruction of Sennacherib," describing how the Assyrian army besieging Jerusalem was wiped out by the plague.

To illuminate different facets of life at the limits, it may be useful to include here a few short poems, inviting the reader to consider how each varies our theme. Shelley wrote one of the most unforgettable sonnets in any language: *Ozymandias*

> I MET a traveler from an antique land
> Who said: Two vast and trunkless legs of stone
> Stand in the desert. Near them on the sand,
> Half sunk, a shatter'd visage lies, whose frown
> And wrinkled lip and sneer of cold command
> Tell that its sculptor well those passions read
> Which yet survive, stamp'd on these lifeless things,
> The hand that mock'd them and the heart that fed;
> And on the pedestal these words appear:
> "My name is Ozymandias, king of kings:
> Look at my works, ye Mighty, and despair!"
> Nothing beside remains. Round the decay
> Of that colossal wreck, boundless and bare,
> The lone and level sands stretch far away.

Shelley also wrote "Adonais: An Elegy on the Death of John Keats . . ." as well as a play, *Prometheus Unbound*, whose concluding lines are included in most anthologies of English poetry:

> To suffer woes which Hope thinks infinite;
> To forgive wrongs darker than death or night;
>   To defy Power, which seems omnipotent;
> To love, and bear; to hope till Hope creates
> From its own wreck the thing it contemplates;
>   Neither to change, nor falter, nor repent;
> This, like thy glory, Titan, is to be
> Good, great and joyous, beautiful and free;
> This is alone Life, Joy, Empire, and Victory.

Since Keats, Shelley, and Byron died, still young, in the 1820s, there have been no poets in English of equal stature. Still, there are some peaks that include Edward Fitzgerald's *The Rubáiyát of Omar Kháyyám* which owe their renown not least to the fact that the theme of these terse quatrains is life at the limits.

> Heaven but the Vision of fulfilled Desire,
> And Hell the Shadow of a Soul on fire
>   Cast on the Darkness into which Ourselves
> So late emerged from, shall so soon expire.
>
> The Moving Finger writes; and, having writ,
> Moves on: nor all your Piety nor Wit
>   Shall lure it back to cancel half a Line
> Nor all your Tears wash out a Word of it.

Lord Tennyson never achieved such brevity, and one of his best-known poems, "In Memoriam," suffers from its excessive length. "The Charge of the Light Brigade," a tale of a dreadful carnage, and "Tears, Idle Tears" are mercifully terse. But the most haunting of his short poems is surely:

> Break, break break,
>   On thy cold gray stones, O sea!
> And I would that my tongue could utter
>   The thoughts that arise in me.
>
> O well for the fisherman's boy
>   That he shouts with his sister at play!
> O well for the sailor lad
>   That he sings in his boat on the bay!
>
> And the stately ships go on,
>   To the haven under the hill;
> But O for the touch of a vanished hand,
>   And the sound of a voice that is still!
>
> Break, break, break,
>   At the foot of thy crags, O sea!
> But the tender grace of a day that is dead
>   Will never come back to me.

Robert Browning was at his best in longer poems, and Matthew Arnold did not write many first-rate poems at all; but in 1867 he published one poem that is perhaps as fine as any written in English since then:

Dover Beach

The sea is calm to-night.
The tide is full, the moon lies fair
Upon the straits;—on the French coast the light
Gleams and is gone; the cliffs of England stand,
Glimmering and vast, out in the tranquil bay.
Come to the window, sweet is the night air!
Only, from the long line of spray
Where the sea meets the moon-blanched land,
Listen! you hear the grating roar
Of pebbles which the waves draw back, and fling,
At their return, up the high strand,
Begin, and cease, and then again begin,
With tremulous cadence slow, and bring
The eternal note of sadness in.

Sophocles long ago
Heard it on the Ægæan, and it brought
Into his mind the turbid ebb and flow
Of human misery; we
Find also in the sound a thought,
Hearing it by this distant northern sea.

The Sea of Faith
Was once, too, at the full, and round earth's shore
Lay like the folds of a bright girdle furled.
But now I only hear
Its melancholy, long, withdrawing roar,
Retreating, to the breath
Of the night wind, down the vast edges near
And naked shingles of the world.

Ah, love, let us be true
To one another! for the world, which seems
To lie before us like a land of dreams,
So various, so beautiful, so new,
Hath really neither joy, nor love, nor light,
Nor certitude, nor peace, nor help for pain;
And we are here as on a darkling plain
Swept with confused alarms of struggle and flight
Where ignorant armies clash by night.

Like most of the other great English poets before him, Arnold sounds the theme of love, but as in them it is not a love pretty like flowers and butterflies; it is love in the midst of the "ebb and flow of human misery." In Oscar Wilde's "The Ballad of Reading Gaol," published at the end of the century, a prisoner is hanged for killing the woman he loved,

yet each man kills the thing he loves . . .

A little later Rudyard Kipling wrote a shorter ballad on the hanging of Danny Deever, and his other short ballads are not much more cheerful.

Born the same year as Kipling, William Butler Yeats returned to the ancient theme of "Agamemnon dead" in what may well be his most perfect poem, "Leda and the Swan." His cycles of poems include "Upon a Dying Lady" and "Meditations in Time of Civil War," as well as his poems on "Crazy Jane" and two dealing with age. In "Sailing to Byzantium" and "Byzantium" the relation of art to age and decay becomes as central as it was in Shakespeare's sonnets.

8

Among American poets Edgar Allan Poe has unquestionably left a mark on literature in other languages, and perhaps Whitman has, too. Both lived their poetry, lived at the brink. Poe is actually best known as a writer of tales that an editor once arranged under such headings as "Tales of Terror," "of Death," and "of Revenge and Murder." Terror also looms large in his verse. Though the things that Poe attempted to do with language and the extent to which he carried onomatopoeia, creating a music of moods, were highly original, he was still easier to assimilate to European traditions than Whitman. Poe's employment of art and stylization meet eye and ear, while Whitman came closer to breaking down the barriers dividing art from reality, life from poetry. His free verse is also stylized but at times seems to be his very breath and unchanneled stream of thought.

Twentieth-century American poets have bettered Whitman's instruction—not only Allen Ginsberg and other beat poets who were in rebellion against academia but also the poets more widely taught in American colleges. Madness and suicide ceased to be merely poetic subjects. Some of the most admired poets created their verse between bouts of derangement, and many ended as suicides. The academic establishment moved so far from the vogue of T. S. Eliot's fastidiousness, which still prevailed for at least a decade after World War II, that during the next two decades madness or suicide almost became prerequisites for poets to be taken *very* seriously. Ezra Pound, Theodore Roethke, Robert Lowell, John Berryman, Sylvia Plath, and Anne Sexton are cases in point, and Plath was not admitted into the pantheon until she had killed herself.

The so-called new criticism that flourished under the aegis of Eliot insisted on the irrelevance of a poet's life to his art. It considered a poem autonomous and ruled out of court not only the biographical and historical context but even a poet's other works. The poem had to be read as if only this poem and nothing else existed. It is understandable that such extreme myopia should have given way to the opposite extreme, but there is still something barbarous about a taste that needs to be titillated by sensational biographical data. For such a taste even trivial poems take on an added glow if the poet himself knew madness, whether that is relevant to the poem or not. What is wanted is some confirmation that our society or "the establishment," if not the world, is rotten, and that the writer could not be reconciled with it. Yet Sophocles, who was utterly sane and lived to the age of ninety, wrote poetry of madness, despair, and suicide second to none.

Madness and suicide are no objections, and Hölderlin, Nietzsche, Van Gogh, and Celan will soon be considered. But the predilection for second-raters whose lives or deaths are sensational is on a par with the widespread confusion of those who think boredom must be communicated by means of boredom. Art is not a mirror that shows reality "like it is." Art shows us a world reflected by an uncommon mind that imposes a style on what it portrays.

9

Even the few poems cited here call into question not only existentialist disquisitions about extreme situations but also the adequacy of the two tables offered in the Prologue. To be sure, "Ozymandias" deals with decay, and the concluding lines of *Prometheus Unbound* celebrate defiance, while the Tennyson poem is on death. Yet the underlying theme of several of these poems, and most obviously of "The Moving Finger writes," is the relentlessness of time. That theme will be explored in depth in *Time Is an Artist*. And it would be premature at this point, so early in our quest, to make a final judgment about the twenty-four categories of the Prologue. We merely should bear in mind as we read the poems in this chapter and consider works of art later on whether any predominantly conceptual approach does not perhaps have serious limitations.

To gain a fuller understanding of the many facets of life at the limits it may be useful to consider at least one altogether different tradition. In German poetry the confrontation with death is a central theme. All the major poets from the seventeenth century to the present have dealt with it in short poems that are widely acclaimed as among the best in the language. Remarkably, none of these poems voices the dread of death, which so many writers consider universal. Some of the poets let on that they, too, have heard such claims, but all of them face death without anxiety.*

It should suffice here to quote only two poets on death: Nietzsche and Hölderlin. Both died insane. Of the other major German poets who wrote enduring poems on death, Trakl and Celan committed suicide, Trakl during World War I, Celan after World War II, after surviving Auschwitz. Trakl had suffered depressions before, but killed himself after surviving a battle and having

---

* See my "Death without Dread" in *Existentialism, Religion, and Death* and my *Twenty-five German Poets.* Except for Celan's "Death Fugue" and three Rilke poems, for which the sources are given in the text, all the German poems quoted or discussed in this chapter are included in the latter volume.

to look after ninety severely wounded men whom he was unable to help. His poems are very short, unpretentious, and beautiful. Celan's "Death Fugue" deals with Auschwitz and is as sane as Nietzsche's and Hölderlin's poems on death. Nietzsche's begins:

> Not long will you thirst,
>   burnt out heart!
> A promise is in the air,
> from unknown lips it blows at me
>   —the great chill comes.

And it ends:

> *Seventh* loneliness!
>   Never felt I
> nearer me sweet security,
> warmer the sun's eye.
> Does not the ice of my peaks still glow?
>   Silver, light, a fish
>   my bark now swims out.

Hölderlin's "To the Parcae" is terse enough to be quoted in full.

To the Parcae

> A single summer grant me, great powers, and
> a single autumn for fully ripened song
>   that, sated with the sweetness of my
>   playing, my heart may more willingly die.
>
> The soul that, living, did not attain its divine
> right cannot repose in the nether world.
>   But once what I am bent on, what is
>   holy, my poetry, is accomplished:
>
> Be welcome then, stillness of the shadows' world!
> I shall be satisfied though my lyre will not
>   accompany me down there. Once I
>   lived like the gods, and more is not needed.

Every one of these poems portrays life at the limits. But a social conscience emerges only on the eve of World War I. In 1912 Gottfried Benn, a doctor, published his first book of verse, *Morgue*, and then also, after his mother had died of cancer, the poem "Man and Woman Walk Through the Cancer Ward." Here we encounter a new, totally unromantic attitude that many critics believe emerged only during the war, a few years later. Here Benn goes way beyond the stylistic advances of Hemingway and of Brecht in the twenties.

A social conscience is also central in a sonnet that Franz Werfel included in a collection of verse in 1913, but here the mood is liberal and sentimental, not lean and icy like Benn's.

When You Enraptured Me

> When my eyes filled, by your presence possessed,
> and thanks to you I soared through the untold,
> was not that day felt by the sick and old,
> by millions that were cruelly oppressed?
>
> When you enraptured me till death seemed best,
> toil was around us, noise, decay, and mold,
> and emptiness, and godless ones were cold;
> men lived and died that never had been blessed.
>
> When you had swelled me till my senses swirled
> and I could fly, the musty dark was teeming,
> at desks men shriveled, and the mills were steaming.
>
> You that on roads and rivers chafe and fret:
> if there is any balance in the world,
> how shall I have to pay this guilty debt?

10

In American poetry the social conscience—outrage in the face of the misery of so many of our fellow men—found eloquent expression much earlier, in 1899, when Edwin Markham published:

The Man with the Hoe

WRITTEN AFTER SEEING MILLET'S WORLD-FAMOUS PAINTING OF A
BRUTALIZED TOILER IN THE DEEP ABYSS OF LABOR.

God made man in his own image:
in the image of God He made him.
—GENESIS.

Bowed by the weight of centuries he leans
Upon his hoe and gazes on the ground,
The emptiness of ages in his face,
And on his back the burden of the world.
Who made him dead to rapture and despair,
A thing that grieves not and that never hopes,
Stolid and stunned, a brother to the ox?
Who loosened and let down this brutal jaw?
Whose was the hand that slanted back this brow?
Whose breath blew out the light within this brain?

Is this the Thing the Lord God made and gave
To have dominion over sea and land;
To trace the stars and search the heavens for power;
To feel the passion of Eternity?
Is this the dream He dreamed who shaped the suns
And markt their ways upon the ancient deep?
Down all the caverns of Hell to their last gulf
There is no shape more terrible than this——
More tongued with cries against the world's blind greed——
More filled with signs and portents for the soul—
More packt with danger to the universe.

What gulfs between him and the seraphim!
Slave of the wheel of labor what to him
Are Plato and the swing of Pleiades?
What the long reaches of the peaks of song,
The rift of dawn, the reddening of the rose?
Thru this dread shape the suffering ages look;
Time's tragedy is in that aching stoop;
Thru this dread shape humanity betrayed,
Plundered, profaned and disinherited,
Cries protest to the Powers that made the world,
A protest that is also prophecy.

O masters, lords and rulers in all lands,
Is this the handiwork you give to God,
This monstrous thing distorted and soul-quencht?
How will you ever straighten up this shape;
Touch it again with immortality;
Give back the upward looking and the light;
Rebuild in it the music and the dream;
Make right the immemorial infamies,
Perfidious wrongs, immedicable woes?

O masters, lords and rulers in all lands,
How will the future reckon with this Man?
How answer his brute question in that hour
When whirlwinds of rebellion shake all shores?
How will it be with kingdoms and with kings—
With those who shaped him to the thing he is—
When this dumb Terror shall rise to judge the world,
After the silence of the centuries?

The poem would be still more powerful if it were shorter. But it marks the beginning of a new genre that was perfected—in the United States, too—on the eve of World War I. In 1913 Vachel Lindsay showed how much a good poet can say in eight lines:

The Leaden-Eyed

Let not young souls be smothered out before
They do quaint deeds and fully flaunt their pride.
It is the world's one crime its babes grow dull,
Its poor are ox-like, limp and leaden-eyed.

Not that they starve, but starve so dreamlessly,
Not that they sow, but that they seldom reap,
Not that they serve, but have no gods to serve,
Not that they die but that they die like sheep.

A year later Louis Untermeyer laced a similar outcry with sarcasm:

Caliban in the Coal Mines

God, we don't like to complain;
    We know that the mine is no lark.
But—there's the pools from the rain;
    But—there's the cold and the dark.

God, You don't know what it is—
    You, in Your well-lighted sky—
Watching the meteors whizz;
    Warm, with a sun always by.

God, if You had but the moon
    Stuck in Your cap for a lamp,
Even You'd tire of it soon,
    Down in the dark and the damp.

Nothing but blackness above
    And nothing that moves but the cars. . . .
God, if You wish for our love,
    Fling us a handful of stars!

It is odd how late the social conscience emerged in the short poem. In art it had surfaced a hundred years earlier in the etchings of Goya. In the novel it was central in Victor Hugo and Charles Dickens no less than in Dostoevsky and Tolstoy. In the theater Bertolt Brecht, in the 1920s, made preposterous claims about his own originality, as if previous playwrights had merely offered their audiences emotional relief and he were the first who made playgoers think and find fault with society; and these untruths have been repeated again and again. On the stage social criticism had been at home almost from the start. Those who do not find it in Aeschylus cannot deny its central role in Euripides and Aristophanes. In this respect as in many others Shakespeare is an exception.

In Germany, where Brecht's advertisements for himself should have been laughed out of court, the theater was an educational institution from the start, and nobody ever failed to see that Lessing's *Nathan der Weise* (1779) was a play that was meant to educate the audience or—in a later phrase—to raise their consciousness. Friedrich Schiller (1759–1805) quite explicitly conceived his mission as a playwright in the same terms, even if he was far less witty than Lessing and occasionally struck a pompous tone that seems dated. Closer to Brecht's own time, there had been Ibsen, Shaw, and Gerhart Hauptmann. Brecht had a marvelous sense of theater, and *Mutter Courage* and *Der kaukasische Kreidekreis* were immensely effective when he staged them, but his originality as a writer has been vastly exaggerated.

Erich Kästner is best known for his children's books in which his social conscience meets the eye; above all, *Emil und die Detektive*. But during the years between World War I and the advent of Hitler, he also created a new kind of light verse, putting forward his critique of society in extremely sarcastic short poems. Others made similar attempts; he did it best.

More than thirty years later, poems of social protest became trendy, and what is trendy rarely lasts. Instead of singling out a few that are memorable and approximating a catalogue, it will be more fruitful to consider in some depth a single poet—perhaps the greatest of the last hundred years: Rainer Maria Rilke.*

11

It is easy to feel irritated by Rilke. He seems remote from the horrors of two world wars. Unlike Kafka, who was also born in Prague, a mere eight years after Rilke, the poet may well seem to have had no feeling for life at the limits. And in the sense in which Solzhenitsyn or Goya dealt with this theme, Rilke did not. But a closer examination of his poetry should add greatly to our understanding of life at the limits.

Many of Rilke's poems are not very good. But poets have to be judged by their best works, and very few poets in any language have given us as many splendid poems as Rilke has.

He does not come across as an exemplary human being—as a representative figure of almost mythical stature—like Goethe or Heine, Nietzsche or Freud. Although his only major prose work, *Malte Laurids Brigge* (1910), was a revolutionary novel that explored new ways of writing, any claim that as a human being he ranks with the men just mentioned would have to be based on his letters. They fill many volumes, and some of his letters are very beautiful. Yet the person who emerges from these volumes is weak, often precious, and disconcertingly lacking in humor.

Many of his poems are also marred by affectations and remind us of the fact that, when he began to publish, the *Jugendstil*, also known as *art nouveau*, was in vogue. Even some of his best poems narrowly miss self-parody. But they do miss it.

The distinction between Rilke as a human being and his poems may suggest a narrowly aesthetic approach. On the contrary, what needs to be shown is how his finest poems have a human dimension that needs to be felt but is often ignored.

To understand Rilke one has to realize that he celebrated life at the limits. His poetry is not imbued with a social conscience, and at the height of the student revolutions of the late 1960s some "new left" admirers of Brecht sought to dispose of Rilke as the author of the line—in a very early poem—

> *Denn Armut ist ein grosser Glanz aus Innen . . .*
> For poverty is a great splendor from within . . .

If Rilke had stopped writing in April 1903, when this was written, he would be an interesting minor poet, although he was even then celebrating life at the limits.

The line is found in an early collection of his poems, *Das Stunden-Buch, The Book of Hours*, which consists of three "books": "On the Monastic Life," "On Pilgrimage," and "On Poverty and Death." Initially, his repudiation of security and his search for extreme situations led the poet to a glorification of monasticism. His mannered style and a tendency to go on and on, piling up extravagant images, cover up, without hiding successfully, his ignorance of real poverty. To arrive at a halfway sympathetic reading, one needs to think of Saint Francis and of Rilke's slightly later poems on the Buddha, which are very short and far superior.

What makes Rilke one of the greatest poets of all time is certainly not *The Book of Hours*, nor even his ambitious *Duino Elegies* (1923), which have elicited a large body of exegesis. Poetry has become an object of study—of graduate study and post-doctoral research—and difficult poems are attracting disproportionate attention. The kind of difficulty that attracts interpreters and gets taught and written about most is all too often the kind that calls for erudition. In line with the cult of quantity and size that is so notable in other fields, too, long poems and large cycles are often overrated, while short poems—the genre in which Rilke really excelled—are underestimated.

What makes many of his short poems difficult—so much so that they are probably not often understood—is that they deal with experiences that many readers do not recognize. The range of the best of them is rather limited. They are variations on a single theme that is, however, as significant as any theme can be. It is the choice between two modes of existence that might be called intensity and peace; the creative life that involves suffering versus Nirvana; Eros and Thanatos; or in the words of Moses: "Choose life or death this day." It cannot be proved which choice is better, but poets can try to explore experiences and show us what they are like. This is what Rilke did superbly.

---

* An earlier version of these reflections on Rilke appeared in *The Times Literary Supplement*, London, December 5, 1975.

Despite the occasionally disturbing artificiality of his style, his variations on his central theme are not contrived. They spring from a profound need and are anything but random. When they are considered chronologically, we begin to understand Rilke's development as a poet and a human being. And his best poems greatly enlarge our comprehension of life at the limits.

Rilke never was the poet of the slums, of human degradation and oppression. Neither was he the poet of daffodils and larks, of simple pleasures or a life of comfort. What he brought to perfection was the short poem that deals with extreme experiences.

He matured late, and much of his early verse is poor. But with the appearance of the two volumes of his *Neue Gedichte* (1907–1908) he emerged as a major poet. These "new poems" have often been called *Ding Gedichte*, but the best of them are not about *things*; they are about human experiences and revolve around the central choice between peace and life at the limits.

Rilke is not so well known that one needs only to mention the titles of the most relevant poems; one has to quote at least a few poems. My translations aim to capture Rilke's tone as well as his meaning, the tone being part of his meaning.

12

A critic once cited Rilke's "Love Song" (in *Neue Gedichte*) as an example of Rilke's alleged subversion of our traditional values. In this poem "Lovers seek separation, not union," he said, implying that this involved a Nietzschean revaluation of all values.* There is no need here to consider Rilke's crucial relationship to Nietzsche, but the claim that Rilke's "Love Song" inverts our traditional values misses not only the point of this one poem but Rilke's central concern with the alternative of Nirvana and intensity.

> *Love Song*
>
> How could I keep my soul so that it might
> not touch on yours? How could I elevate
>
> it over you to reach to other things?
> Oh, I would like to hide it out of sight
> with something lost in endless darkenings,
> in some remote, still place, so desolate
> it does not sing whenever your depth sings.
> Yet all that touches us, myself and you,
> takes us together like a violin bow
> that draws a single voice out of two strings.
> Upon what instrument have we been strung?
> And who is playing with us in his hand?
> Sweet is the song.

What the poet seeks is peace. But he is far from deaf to the beauty that can come of lack of peace, of an intensity that is scarcely endurable. "Sweet is the song." The experience of love as a source of suffering is by no means new, although it has been emphasized far less in the West than in Buddhism. The Buddha became peace incarnate and taught that love and attachment breed suffering. The first volume of *Neue Gedichte* contains two poems entitled "Buddha," and the second volume ends with "Buddha in the Glory." In his longing for peace Rilke returned to the Buddha again and again.

Perhaps none of Rilke's poems is more famous than his evocation of a caged panther in the Paris zoo.

> *The Panther*
> IN THE JARDIN DES PLANTES, PARIS
>
> His glance, worn by the passing of the bars,
> has grown so weary it has lost its hold.
> It seems to him, there are a thousand bars,
> and then behind a thousand bars no world.
>
> The soft gait of the supple, forceful paces,
> revolving in a circle almost nil,
> is like a dance of power that embraces
> a core containing, dazed, a mighty will.
>
> Rarely the pupil's curtain, soundlessly,
> is raised—and then an image enters him,
> goes through the silent tension of the limbs—
> and in his heart ceases to be.

* Erich Heller, "Rilke and Nietzsche" in *The Disinherited Mind* (1952). For a different view see my "Nietzsche and Rilke" and "Art, Tradition, and Truth," both published originally in 1955 and reprinted in *From Shakespeare to Existentialism* (1959).

It would be silly to suggest that Rilke's poems are designed merely to make a point. But the mistake made much more often in reading Rilke is to overlook that many of his poems also explore a particular experience and raise questions. The panther in his cage has found peace, but is peace really desirable? We are thrown back upon our central theme.

"Orpheus. Eurydice. Hermes" is a very much longer poem, but no less beautiful than "The Panther"; and it deals with the same alternative. The great poet, the unequaled master of the sweet song, descends to the underworld to bring back from the dead his wife:

> The one so loved that from a single lyre
> wails came surpassing any wailing women;
> that out of wails a world arose in which
> all things were there again . . .

But Eurydice has found peace. Hermes accompanies the poet, and on the way back walks with Eurydice. Rilke's poem describes the ascent. Rilke accepts the tradition that if the poet looks back even once, his wife must return to the realm of death. The poem is woven around the contrast between the poet's intensity of which his art is born and the total peace of Eurydice. Orpheus

> looked ahead in silence and impatience.
> His paces, without chewing, gulped the way
> in outsized swallows; . . .
>
> Eurydice   walked at the hand of this great god,
> her striding straightened by the grave's long wraps,
> uncertain, soft, and void of all impatience.

She has found peace, and anyone who brought her back into this world would not do her a favor. Rilke's evocation of the other world in which—in the words of a spiritual that Marian Anderson used to sing—"all is peace" has never been surpassed. Though long, the poem is not too long; it sustains its mood and central contrast without flagging and ends beautifully.

Even so those who come to Rilke with entirely different experiences and problems often miss his theme. Robert Lowell, for example, says in the Introduction to his *Imitations* that "in poetry tone is of course everything. I have been reckless with literal meaning, and labored hard to get the tone." Yet his version of the Orpheus poem ends:

> the reproachful god of messengers
> looking round, pushed off again.
> His caduceus was like a shotgun on his shoulder.

Rilke's poem ends, repeating two lines used earlier to describe Eurydice's ascent, which are equally appropriate to her descent:

> with sorrow in his eyes, the god of message
> turned silently to follow back the form
> that even then returned this very way,
> her striding straightened by the grave's long wraps,
> uncertain, soft, and void of all impatience.

In this poem peace is reaffirmed, but this is not Rilke's last word. He kept wrestling with the tension between life at the limits and peace.

The Orpheus poem stands near the end of the first volume of *Neue Gedichte*. The second volume opens with

Archaic Torso of Apollo

> We did not know his high, unheard-of head
> where his eyes' apples ripened. Yet his torso has
> retained their glowing as
> a candelabrum where his vision, not yet dead,
>
> only turned low, still shines. For else the breast
> could not blind you, nor could we still discern
> the smile that wanders in the loins' faint turn
> to that core which once carried manhood's crest.
>
> Else would this stone, disfigured and too small,
> stand mute under the shoulders' lucid fall,
> and not gleam like a great cat's skin, and not
>
> burst out of all its contours, bright
> as a great star: there is no spot
> that does not see you. You must change your life.

Here intensity is celebrated and desired. The challenge of the Greek torso is no longer that of the Buddha. Our lives are lacking in intensity. But intensity is nothing like busyness; it is embodied in a headless piece of stone. Still, the stone is not dead; it is glowing and introduces the imagery of burning into our theme.

As one turns the page from "Archaic Torso," one encounters "Leda," a poem that invites comparison with William Butler Yeats' "Leda and the Swan," published fifteen years later, in 1923. Yeats' poem is violent, Leda is raped, and "The broken wall" brings to mind "the burning roof and tower / And Agamemnon dead." The terror of the girl's rape extends far beyond her, and as soon as "the brute blood of the air" has had his pleasure with her "the indifferent beak could let her drop"; as soon as the passion is spent, it is all over and the poem ends.

Rilke's version of the same myth is as different as can be. It is devoid of violence. Even where that may seem to be called for by the story, Rilke chooses to dispense with it; and nothing could be more alien to his tone and temper than a "shotgun" in the last line of "Orpheus. Eurydice. Hermes." Rilke is soft to a fault. But in "Leda" as in the Orpheus poem and in all of his best verse, the softness is no fault. His "Leda" ends:

> He came down, smooth and white,
> and sliding his neck through her weakening hand,
>
> he loosed his godhead in her loveliness—
> then only felt his feathers' full delight
> and truly became swan in her caress.

In Rilke's poem the real climax comes after the sexual climax, after the passion is spent. The most intense experience is discovered to be compatible with peace.

13

Two years later Rilke published *Malte Laurids Brigge*, and another two years later, in 1912, he began his *Elegies* but found himself unable to finish them. During the World War he was devastated and fell silent. Only the fourth elegy, which is not one of the better ones, was written during the war, in 1915.

On the last day of January 1922 the ice finally broke and Rilke's soul was set free again. Perhaps no other poet has ever experienced such a storm of inspiration. In February Rilke was able to complete his *Duino Elegies*, writing the fifth, seventh, and eighth from scratch, and composing much of the ninth as well; and between February 2 and 5 he also wrote the twenty-six *Sonnets to Orpheus* that comprise Part One, while the twenty-nine of Part Two were written between February 15 and 23.

The short poems Rilke wrote during this period are easily as remarkable as his *Elegies*. In fact, the *Elegies* were begun in 1912 and could be offered as a unit, although the material written in February 1922 is generally far superior to the earlier parts. In the short poems, however, Rilke found an altogether new voice that differs sharply from his earlier poems. While the *Sonnets to Orpheus* were the last volume of German poems Rilke himself published, he wrote other short poems in more or less the same voice until about two weeks before he died. These late short poems bring to mind some of the verse of the old Goethe, even as the *Elegies* bring to mind Nietzsche's "Dionysus Dithyrambs"; but Rilke's style, especially in the short poems, is quite distinctive.

Rather oddly, Gottfried Benn (1886–1956), whose early poems—for example *Morgue* and "Man and Woman Walk Through the Cancer Ward"—were about as different from Rilke's as can be, imitated Rilke's later voice in his own later poems, beginning in the late thirties. Actually, Rilke was probably in the back of Benn's mind from the beginning. Rilke had used the title "Morgue" for a poem in his *Neue Gedichte*, and Benn surely felt that this subject called for an altogether different style. But his late verse is plainly derivative from Rilke's late poems, which were revolutionary.

Although Rilke found a new tone, Rilke's central theme remained unchanged. To show this, one could cite a very large number of poems, but it will suffice here to consider a very few, beginning with the poem that marks the breakthrough to the final period. Rilke wrote it into a collection of his early verse, as a dedication for Nanny Wunderly-Volkart, whom he called Nike. The poem was published posthumously and is to be found in *Sämtliche Werke* (volume II, page 132). In German it begins: "*Solang du Selbstgeworfnes fängst . . .*"

Nike

(Muzot, on the last day of January 1922)

As long as you are catching *your* throws, all
is skill and trivial gain. Only when you
have suddenly caught in your hands the ball
that an eternal female partner threw
right at your core in a trajectory
that is an arch in God's vast edifice—
then is ability to catch, a glory—
not yours, a world's. And if you should possess
the strength and daring to return the shot—
no, still more wonderful, if you forgot
daring and strength and had already hurled
the ball—(as an old year throws swarms
of migratory birds across the world
that aging warmth tosses to youthful warmth)—
then only, in such risks, your playing matters.
Now you no longer try for easy prizes,
nor do you strain for what is hard and flatters
your prowess. Out of your hand rises
the meteor and speeds into its spaces.

As so often in Rilke's late short poems, the syntax and thought are complex and so different from what most readers expect to find in poetry that his verse may seem inaccessible. But the theme traced here provides an entry. Forget daring and strength, forget yourself, cease straining, be ready. And suddenly the ball may be yours, and you no longer think, plan, or exert yourself:

Out of your hands rises
the meteor and speeds into its spaces.

What meteor? The poem. It is no longer *your* poem, your work, but a cosmic explosion—a spark that nature struck from you, but suddenly it is not some small spark but something vast that leaves your hands and stuns large numbers of people whom you never knew.

Rilke had lived with the symbol of the ball for a long time. We encounter it, for example, in one of the finest poems in his early volume, *Das Buch der Bilder* (1902), in "The Song of the Idiot":

Look at that ball, isn't it fair—
red and round as an everywhere.
Good you created the ball.
Whether it comes when we call?

Only an idiot would think that it does, and Rilke had long learned to his sorrow how it does not come by being summoned or craved. But when it did come, he was ready for it.

14

In *Sonnets to Orpheus* our theme remains central. In the third sonnet it is particularly accessible.

A god can do it. But how can one follow,
mere man, oh, tell me, through the narrow art?
Man's sense is discord. Where ways of the heart
are crossing stands no temple for Apollo.

Song, as you teach it, does not reach nor yearn,
nor does it woo what is at last attained;
song is existence. For the god, unstrained.
But when do we exist? When will he turn,

to help us to exist, the earth and sky?
It is not this, youth, that you love, although
your voice then opens up your lips—oh, try

forgetting that you ever sang. That flees.
Singing in truth is breath that does not flow.
An aimless breath. Suspense in god. A breeze.

Of the many other sonnets in which this theme is developed it will suffice to mention the twelfth of Part Two, which begins:

> Choose to be changed. Oh experience the rapture of fire
> in which a life is concealed, exulting in change as it burns;
> and the projecting spirit who is master of the entire
> earth loves the figure's flight less than the point where it turns.

Here the motif of burning is fused with the imagery of flight and conversion, and the poem ends:

> And Daphne, since her transformation
> into a baytree, desires that you choose to be changed into wind.

Still, you must change your life and choose to be changed—but not into something in particular that you desire. Rather it is a matter of not locking yourself up, of not being rigid, of becoming fluid and squandering yourself. The last words of the two sonnets cited here are the same in the original German: *Wind*. The meaning of that image is spelled out in a dedicatory poem of 1924: having no hiding place; being shelterless, living dangerously without any preconceived goal.* In these late poems the fusion of peace and intensity is attained.

Both the *Elegies* and the *Sonnets* were published in 1923, and at the end of the year Rilke wrote another dedication for "Nike" into a copy of the *Elegies*. (The German text, which begins "*Alle die Stimmen der Bäche*," appears in *Sämtliche Werke*, vol. II, pp. 256f.)

It may be possible to read this poem, especially in the German original, without even noticing the image that is crucial. In German the poem ends:

> *aber, statt dass es schwinde,*
> *steht es im Glühn der Erhörung*
>
> *singend und unversehrt.*

This is surely an allusion to the story of Moses and the burning bush: "the bush was burning, yet it was not consumed."

For Nike

(Christmas 1923)

All of the streams' countless voices,	Oh, I know, I feel sure,
every drop from the rock,	names and their nature and need;
as the cycle rejoices,	inside of what is mature
to the god I give back,	rests the original seed,
trembling with weak arms, and glow.	only increased and illumed.
Sudden breezes, though mild,	Hoping for something divine,
were for me omen or fright,	rises, to conjure, the word,
every profound insight	and it refuses to wane,
made me again a child—	burning as it is heard,
and I felt that I know.	singing and not consumed.

Line ten borders on self-parody: "*und ich fühlte: ich weiss.*" Indeed, this poem was not written all at once. The first twelve lines had been completed in the first days of February 1922, and the rest had been added just before Christmas 1923. The bulk of this poem may be seen as a prelude to the last two lines, and the whole poem as a prelude to the last entry in Rilke's last notebook, probably written in mid-December 1926, about two weeks before Rilke died of leukemia on December 29. (*Sämtliche Werke*, vol. II, p. 511.) Here his abandonment has become total; there is no hiding place, no shelter, no effort, no memories, as the poet burns to death, singing.

There are many poems about death, many kinds of death, not many poems about cancer, none like this. It was born of a lifelong exploration of one of the greatest themes with which a poet could deal: the tension between peace and intensity, between the serenity of the Buddha and the challenge of an archaic torso of Apollo. And when nature hurled leukemia at the poet, he was ready and responded:

---

* *Sämtliche Werke*, vol. II, p. 261; *Twenty-five German Poets*, pp. 248f.

Komm du, du letzter, den ich anerkenne,
heilloser Schmerz im leiblichen Geweb:
wie ich im Geiste brannte, sieh, ich brenne
in dir; das Holz hat lange widerstrebt,

der Flamme, die du loderst, zuzustimmen,
nun aber nähr' ich dich und brenn in dir.
Mein hiesig Mildsein wird in deinem Grimmen
ein Grimm der Hölle nicht von hier.

Ganz rein, ganz planlos frei von Zukunft stieg
ich auf des Leidens wirren Scheiterhaufen,
so sicher nirgend Künftiges zu kaufen
um dieses Herz, darin der Vorrat schwieg.

Bin ich es noch, der da unkenntlich brennt?
Erinnerungen reiß ich nicht herein.
O Leben, Leben: Draußensein.
Und ich in Lohe. Niemand der mich kennt.

You are the last I recognize; return,
pain beyond help that sears the body's cells:
as I burnt in the spirit, see, I burn
in you; the wood, that for so long rebels

against the flame you kindle, comes of age;
behold, I nourish you and burn in you.
My earthly mildness changes in your rage
into a rage of hell I never knew.

Quite pure, quite planless, of all future free,
I climbed the stake of suffering, resolute
not to acquire what is still to be
to clad this heart whose stores had become mute.

Is it still I that burns there all alone?
Unrecognizable? memories denied?
O life, O life: being outside.
And I in flames—no one is left—unknown.

There is much that a "new critic" could tell us about this poem while ignoring the fact that it was written by a dying man. Rilke's mannerism may even invite an excessively aesthetic approach. But his last poem as well as the others cited here have a dimension too often ignored by Rilke's readers: a philosophical dimension. What is needed is the discovery of the poet's experience of life, through his works which need to be seen as stages in a development. "*Komm du, du letzter, den ich anerkenne*" marks the end of a road. And one understands the poem better when one has followed this road.

15

Looking back now, we recall that European literature begins with the death of kings in the *Iliad*, but Homer does not choose to tell "sad stories." He uses inherently depressing material—the carnage in a war fought over a woman who was not worth it—to make of it a work of art whose beauty has enchanted generations. Greek tragedy was inspired by Homer, as the Greeks always knew, but in some, though not all, of the finest Greek tragedies the sufferings of a single heroine or hero were moved into the center. Actually, something very much like this had been done earlier in the *Odyssey*.

Tragedy has remained true to this pattern, for the most part, down to modern times. In this respect Shakespeare was still close to Homer and to Greek tragedy. In the eighteenth century first Lessing and then Schiller departed from tradition by writing tragedies with heroines or heroes that were neither kings nor queens nor nobles, and these plays voiced social protest, but no more so than some of Euripides' tragedies: for example, *The Trojan Women*.

The novel has also stayed in the ancient mold. Like Homer, it brings before us a whole society but usually focuses on the sufferings of a few individuals, sometimes of a single hero or heroine, and the object is not to depress but to entertain and, more rarely, to communicate a distinctive experience of life. Where adventure predominates, we are closer to the *Odyssey* than to the *Iliad*, but the basic intent remains Homeric: to make suffering beautiful.

The modern novel, it may be objected, is really different. Solzhenitsyn, of course, is not, though he writes with a more than Tolstoyan sense of moral outrage—like Euripides. But the avant-garde novel created by Joyce may seem to be a really new beginning, yet James Joyce did not call his novel *Ulysses* for nothing. More than any great novel before his, it cannot even be understood without a detailed knowledge of Homer. We are offered an Irish Telemachus and an Odysseus who is a twentieth-century Irish Jew, and still we witness their tribulations transfigured by the magnificent language of a man who was always as much a poet as he was a novelist.

Short poems do not allow a writer to sketch a society or even to invent and flesh out unforgettable characters. Occasionally, a short poem moves a familiar hero into a new light; but typically this genre is a vehicle for expressing the poet's own feelings, thoughts, or experiences, and even when he does not mention himself—and he usually doesn't—he is the hero whose suffering, despair, or confrontation with death is sung.

Successful exceptions are rare. To "The Man with the Hoe," "The Leaden-Eyed," and "Caliban in the Coal Mines" one could hardly add many written before 1914. Rilke's attempts in "The

Voices," which he added in the second edition of his *Book of Images* (*Buch der Bilder*) in 1906, to give voice to a beggar, a blind man, a drunk, a suicide, a widow, an idiot, an orphan, a dwarf, and a leper, are remarkable but do not compare with the heights he reached later. And in his final month he consummated the development begun in ancient Greece by Homer and sang not only his own suffering but his death.

Short poems about the sufferings of others are rarely if ever as splendid as Shakespeare's sonnets about his own despair, or Milton's about his blindness, or Rilke's poem about his dying. Let those who feel the torments of others as keenly as these poets felt their own take heart! What they are burning to say has not been pre-empted. But one of the reasons for that is that poems of this kind are harder to write.

No poem has ever given me more trouble than this, finished finally in 1961 and included in *Cain:*

Portrait of a Lady
Interrogation Center in Germany, 1945

I

With bleakly pleading eyes she talked
of a tar winter when the rivers froze:
caught by the Germans, she had walked
from wall to wall when it was death to doze,
and could have warmth and food and bed
if she would only tell them what she knew—
and told, and saw men hanged till dead—
and she was raped—but if I were inclined,
that would be different and she would not mind:
who else could help her now but I?
She has no mind but does not want to die.

II

In every cell they tell the same,
as children spell, scared without shame,
and give no picture, dwelling on the frame.
They tell it well, and they are not to blame,
for hell
is not a lake of flame.

III

Was there no time for death? Were they too busy
selling their bodies to the butchers? Why
did she walk back and forth till she was dizzy
and starve and kill if there was time to die?
Was it to tell it now to strangers,
barely listening as they measure
the pleasure
of her breasts against the dangers?

IV

To put down
one stroke that finishes a bold design,
some die content. In hell
she dreaded death. Her body all she has to give,
the burnt-out shell
still craves to live.

V

Outside the spring is pretty,
and the women are nicer outside;
for her likes they have no pity,
and they have a lot more pride.
But when the river was frozen,
how many of them would have chosen
torture or suicide?
Outside are flowering trees,
and outside people look well.
Inside the rivers still freeze,
inside is the void of hell.

Here we are closer to "The Man with the Hoe" than to Greek tragedy. Life at the limits is not all of a kind, and different plays, epics, novels, and short poems reveal an inexhaustible variety of extreme situations and responses. There is much more to our theme than has been dreamt of by any philosopher.

Willows

The weeping wil
        lows wake and smile
at daffodil
        and snowdrop while
the maples sigh
        and toss and snore
winter must die
        spring's at the door.

Magnolias

The magnolias were boldly
ahead of their season
      crouch and be still
the wind smote them coldly
for no other reason
      the frost did not kill
      the daffodil.

Riot

Spring runs riot
through streets and gardens
trampling compassion
and mocking despair.

III

WESTERN PHILOSOPHY

16

Philosophy is a branch of literature in which suffering and extreme situations have traditionally been largely ignored. It is widely understood that philosophy should help one to bear suffering "philosophically." Philosophy certainly helps one to endure the sufferings of others by distracting one's attention from them. It makes a virtue of callousness.

Being human, many of the major philosophers must have suffered themselves. But most of them do not seem to have suffered very intensely and were evidently able to distract themselves by pursuing philosophy.

It is extraordinary how much Western literature and philosophy have been shaped by the Greeks. Homer, Aeschylus, Sophocles, and Euripides established a home for life at the limits in literature. Socrates, Plato, and Aristotle, who created Western philosophy, included almost everything except life at the limits.

Nowadays few people think of philosophy as a branch of literature. It has become a commonplace that philosophy must emulate science. And if we do not reproach mathematics and physics, astronomy or chemistry for ignoring life at the limits, it may seem unfair to fault philosophy. But it is not.

In the sciences spectacular progress has been made by bold feats of abstraction from the human condition. Philosophy cannot point to any comparable achievements during the last two hundred years. Moreover—and this is crucial—many of the greatest philosophers have dealt after a fashion with the human condition and the question: What is man? In this respect also, Descartes and Spinoza, Leibniz and Hume, Kant and Hegel followed in the footsteps of Plato and Aristotle. But to understand man's lot one cannot ignore life at the limits.

Even the philosophers who made bold to deal with God's purposes remained far from the spirit of the Old Testament and remained in the framework created by Plato and Aristotle. When they touched on human suffering, the point was almost always to show how it fitted into God's wondrous design of the world. Human misery was ignored unless one mentioned it in discussing the problem of evil or what was once called theodicy—the vindication of God. Some lengthy and florid essays say little that cannot be condensed into four lines:

Theodicy

Why did God make hemorrhoids?
To love the light we need the dark
and girls with adenoids
enhance the song of the lark.*

Such imputations of callousness may seem personal, *ad hominem,* and philosophers would rather discuss their efforts as if they were truly scientific. Efforts are not lacking to defend Saint Thomas' proofs of God's existence, but one does not mention that these proofs depend on many more hidden premises than his proof that the Inquisition, which had only just been launched, was right to burn heretics. Granting only the New Testament doctrine that unbelief is punished with eternal damnation, the execution of those who lead others astray makes very good sense.

The point at issue is not *ad hominem.* It concerns not one individual saint only but the impact of Christianity on philosophy and Western attitudes toward man. The most eminent Christians during the Middle Ages accepted Saint Augustine's view that it was sinful to feel compassion for the damned, and many taught that the sight of the torments of hell would be an important part of the bliss of heaven. The sixteenth chapter of Luke was cited in this context, nor could anyone who felt otherwise cite any sayings of Jesus that either commanded or at least expressed compassion for the vast majority of mankind who, according to the Gospels, was either

* From *Cain and Other Poems* (Kaufmann).

headed for eternal tortures or suffering them right then. On the contrary, Mark, Luke, and Matthew reported that Jesus had actually comforted his disciples by assuring them that those who would not heed them would fare even worse than the greatest evildoers of the past. Such notions could scarcely have failed to confirm and increase human callousness. If one felt that way even about agonies endured eternally with no hope of relief, one naturally did not feel squeamish about temporal sufferings. One saw nothing wrong with torturing or burning people, with the bloodbaths of the Albigensian Crusade and the other Crusades, or with slavery, war, and destitution.

Thus religion reinforced the legacy of the Greeks and kept philosophers from exploring life at the limits. When philosophy finally took a new turn in the seventeenth century, it was Descartes who pointed the way, and being a mathematician of genius, he sought to establish a new method derived from mathematics. Ever since, most philosophers have tried to be scientific.

17

Before the rise of positivism in the nineteenth century, no philosopher used the word "science" or *Wissenschaft* more frequently and emphatically than Hegel, who found a place for it in the title of every book he published. It was in response to him that human suffering finally was admitted to a place of honor in philosophy. This development was foreshadowed in 1759 when Voltaire responded to the great earthquake at Lisbon in 1755 by publishing *Candide*, mocking the claim in Leibniz' *Theodicy* that our world is "the best of all possible worlds." But *Candide* had remained a single shot that did not start an epic battle.

Exactly sixty years later, Schopenhauer, who detested Hegel, published *The World as Will and Idea*, which initially met with no response. But Schopenhauer did not have as many strings to his bow as Voltaire. He devoted his life to his "pessimistic" philosophy, and in the 1850s his central emphasis on suffering finally gained wide attention. He stressed his debts to Plato and Kant no less than his opposition to Christianity and to theism generally, and he found the great precedent for his concern with suffering in Buddhism. Thus the two modern philosophers who first derided our philosophical tradition for ignoring human suffering—Voltaire and Schopenhauer —were both militant anti-Christians.

Another response to Hegel and the tradition of Western philosophy was even slower to gain a hearing. In the 1840s Søren Kierkegaard published more than a dozen volumes, including *Fear and Trembling, The Concept of Dread, The Sickness unto Death* (meaning despair), and *Concluding Unscientific Postscript*. He saw science as well as philosophy that aspired to be scientific as distractions from the extreme situations which he considered at length. Kierkegaard saw himself not as a philosopher but as a Christian writer who polemicized against philosophy, and he neither meant to revolutionize philosophy nor did he—until World War I had shaken up Germany to her roots. Only then was he "born posthumously," to use Nietzsche's apt phrase that covers the fate of both men.

The Christian thinker who finally succeeded long after his death in moving extreme situations into the center of philosophical reflection was infinitely more concerned about his own dread and despair than about human misery, and he prevailed only in conjunction with Nietzsche, who had called himself "The Antichrist." Even then Kierkegaard's influence was confined largely to a few philosophers and theologians in Germany. It was only after the defeat of France in World War II that existentialism spread to France, and after the war it became the most widely discussed philosophy of all time, owing to the writings of Jean-Paul Sartre, who made a point of being an atheist. Insofar as Sartre introduced into existentialism a social conscience and a deep concern for suffering humanity, he did this under the influence not of Kierkegaard or any Christian thinker but of Marx.

It is noteworthy that Kierkegaard's interest in life at the limits involved a literary sensibility. To be sure, his literary graces are easily exaggerated. His books often read like parodies of Hegel. Kierkegaard's admirers have claimed that this was intentional. However that may be, Kierkegaard sometimes published more books in a single year than Hegel ever did, and his total oeuvre is so vast that the result is tedious much of the time. Great parodists require no more than a couple of pages to make their point. In some ways the leading British philosophers, from Bacon and Hobbes to Berkeley and Hume, J. S. Mill and Russell, are far better writers. They are certainly incomparably clearer. Yet they did not approximate the imagination of poets and novelists, as

Kierkegaard did, or Sartre. And these two men made as much of life at the limits as many poets and novelists do.

18

Nietzsche was a great poet, and no German philosopher has written better prose. As a student he discovered Schopenhauer and was charmed by his honest insistence on the suffering in the world. Nietzsche's first book, however, *The Birth of Tragedy*, was a proclamation of his emancipation from Schopenhauer. Nietzsche pointed out that the tragic poets of Greece had not closed their eyes to human suffering but had nevertheless celebrated life as beautiful. Tragedy saved Nietzsche from pessimism and from Schopenhauer's negation of life.

Nietzsche probably suffered more than any other major philosopher. He was in great physical pain much of the time and never lost sight of this aspect of life. But he resisted any suggestion that life and the world are evil, and he always aspired to a joyous, Dionysian affirmation of life.

Because he wrote so well, it is tempting to quote a great many passages. But there is one above all others that advances the theme of life at the limits, and it may suffice to cite two sentences from section 283 of *The Gay Science*: "The secret for harvesting from existence the greatest fruitfulness and the greatest enjoyment is—to *live dangerously*! Build your cities on the slopes of Vesuvius!"

Living securely is a paltry thing. But living dangerously does not mean for Nietzsche what Mussolini meant when he quoted these two words. Nietzsche, who called himself "the last anti-political German," was understood better by some of the great poets and novelists who admired him than by the politicians or even by most of the professors who have written about him. The point about living dangerously was understood very well by Rilke, but also by Hermann Hesse and Gottfried Benn, by André Gide and by many others—but not so much by the arch-professorial German existentialists.

To spell out Nietzsche's meaning in a few words is impossible. But one can at least note that the security he spurns includes taking refuge in comfortable old beliefs, in consensuses on faith and morals, in a well-established way of life, in traditional ways of writing, thinking, and feeling. He rejects conformism, including all attempts to be timely or trendy or to seek safety in numbers. Living dangerously means going it alone, questioning every consensus, suspecting whatever is comfortable, being open to new experiences and perspectives, treating one's own experiences like so many experiments, and always having the courage for an attack on one's dearest convictions.

This is a heroic conception of life at the limits that is a far cry from the many heroized portraits in various media that his sister later commissioned and that have gained great popularity. Nietzsche was a philosopher of nuances, not crudities; he was not only a great philosopher and major poet but also a man in whom an exceptional sensitivity was joined to a relentless critical intelligence.

19

German existentialism is *chatter* about life at the limits. Karl Jaspers has the great merit of having coined the word *Grenzsituation(en)*, limit, boundary, or border situation(s) or extreme or ultimate situation(s). Jaspers' own explanation, duly cited in the elaborate Glossary of the Jaspers volume in The Library of Living Philosophers, is characteristically pedestrian and formulaic: "Situations such as the fact that I am always in situations, that I cannot live without conflict and suffering, that I unavoidably incur guilt, that I must die." This ostensive definition suggests little more than human finitude and is a far cry from Nietzsche's conception of living dangerously. Nevertheless, Jaspers' terminology, like many of his central ideas, is derived from Nietzsche.

In section 15 of *The Birth of Tragedy*—an earlier draft of the book ended with that section—Nietzsche says:

> Science, spurred by its powerful illusion, speeds irresistibly towards its limits where its optimism, concealed in the essence of logic, suffers shipwreck. For the periphery of the circle of science has an infinite number of points; and while there is no telling how this circle could ever be surveyed completely, noble and gifted men nevertheless reach, e'er half their time and inevitably, such boundary points on the periphery from which one gazes into what

defies illumination. When they see to their horror how logic coils up at these boundaries and finally bites its own tail—suddenly the new form of insight breaks through, *tragic insight* which, merely to be endured, needs art as a protection and remedy.

The German word for suffering shipwreck is *scheitern,* which was to become one of Jaspers' key terms, and he expanded Nietzsche's boundary points (*Grenzpunkte*) into *Grenzsituationen,* claiming that from these situations one can derive an illumination of existence, one's own possibilities, what one might become.

As a young man, Jaspers discovered that he had a perforated lung, and he expected to die early. Much preoccupied with his mortality, he took such exceedingly good care of himself that he lived to be eighty-six. Through two World Wars and the whole Nazi period he spent most of his life at his desk, writing book after book, and all of them breathe an exceedingly sheltered atmosphere and are very remote from life—not to speak of life at the limits.

Martin Heidegger, the other representative of German existentialism, is thought widely to have lived on a mountain. In fact, he lived in a suburban house and also had a cottage in nearby Todtnauberg which, although *Berg* means mountain and *Tod* means death, is merely a village. And his disquisitions on death and Being-toward-death and fearless resolution are, to quote Hamlet, "words, words, words." His health also kept him home in 1914. He was no pacifist, but by being careful he also lived to be eighty-six. During World War I, while almost his whole generation was at the front, he began his academic career. His dissertation appeared in 1914, the essay required for commencing a teaching career in 1916, and another short article the same year. On this basis he became a full professor. He became popular with students because he could generate great excitement and talked about things that were timely, like death and resoluteness, guilt and anxiety, being authentic and inauthentic. He claimed that all this was a way of getting at the meaning of Being. But he spoke like a scholastic, not as a poet; the content seemed to be that of the poets and novelists of the time, but the voice was always extremely academic, and the arguments always depended on words, words, words.

He had an academic chair, but after ten years, as he himself later recalled it in print (in "My Way to Phenomenology"), "the dean of the philosophical faculty in Marburg" told him: "Professor Heidegger—you have got to publish something now. Do you have a manuscript?" It was a matter of obtaining a more prestigious chair, and for the sake of that "I had to submit my closely protected work to the public." What was finished of it was rushed into print and appeared in 1927 as *Sein und Zeit: Erste Hälfte* (*Being and Time: First Half*), complete with copious remarks about what would be done in the later parts—and also with such passages as this: "whoever 'is on the track of something' in a genuine manner does not talk about it." Heidegger got the chair, and the rest of the work never appeared.

With his glaring lack of any sense of humor, any wit, any light touch, he was essentially a comic figure. But many academic types who did not trust Nietzsche or literature, being unable to stomach what was not respectably academic, discovered some issues related to life at the limits through Heidegger.

No sooner had Hitler come to power than the apostle of resolute Being-toward-death accepted the rectorship of his university and proclaimed that labor service and military service were not enough; we must also enter "the knowledge service" of the Third Reich and banish academic freedom "from the German university." This summons was presented in the form of a disquisition on "the essence of science" that is no different in the form of argument from his more widely admired philosophical books.* A conception of life at the limits that involves genuine risk might have passed Heidegger's understanding.

After 1945 he claimed occasionally that as early as 1934 he had become disillusioned with Hitler. It does not seem to have occurred to him that in some ways this claim made matters worse. Where was his resoluteness? He made a point of claiming in 1953 when he published his *Introduction to Metaphysics,* originally presented in the form of lectures in 1935, that a passage referring to "the inner truth and greatness of this movement" was ambiguous. Since the phrase occurred only one line after a reference to National Socialism, which was then known in Germany as "the movement," his listeners had naturally assumed that this was what he meant. But

---

* *Die Selbstbehauptung der deutschen Universität,* 1933, pp. 15–20.

Heidegger, who in *Being and Time* had singled out chatter, ambiguity, and curiosity as the three categories of inauthenticity, took pride in claiming that what he had meant even then was an altogether different movement. German existentialism is *chatter* about life at the limits.

20

Months later, when I rarely saw the Angels, I still had the legacy of the big machine—four hundred pounds of chrome (. . .) My first crash had wrecked the bike completely and it took several months to have it rebuilt. (. . .)

So it was always at night, like a werewolf, that I would take the thing out for an honest run down the coast. I would start in Golden Gate Park, thinking only to run a few long curves to clear my head . . . but in a matter of minutes I'd be out at the beach with the sound of the engine in my ears, the surf booming up on the sea wall and a fine empty road stretching all the way down to Santa Cruz (. . .)

There was no helmet on those nights, no speed limit, and no cooling it down on the curves. The momentary freedom of the park was like the one unlucky drink that shoves a wavering alcoholic off the wagon. I would come out of the park near the soccer field (. . .)

Then into first gear, forgetting the cars (. . .) then into second (. . .) then into third, the boomer gear, pushing seventy-five and the beginning of a windscream in the ears, a pressure on the eyeballs like diving into water off a high board.

Bent forward, far back on the seat, and a rigid grip on the handlebars as the bike starts jumping and wavering in the wind. Taillights far up ahead coming closer, faster, and suddenly—zaaapppp—going past and leaning down for a curve near the zoo, where the road swings out to sea.

The dunes are flatter here, and on windy days sand blows across the highway, piling up in thick drifts as deadly as any oil-slick . . . instant loss of control, a crashing, cartwheeling slide and maybe one of those two-inch notices in the paper next day: "An unidentified motorcyclist was killed last night when he failed to negotiate a turn on Highway I."

Indeed . . . but no sand this time, so the lever goes up into fourth, and now there's no sound except wind. (. . .) raise the headlight beam, the needle leans down on a hundred, and wind-burned eyeballs strain to see down the centerline, trying to provide a margin for the reflexes.

But with the throttle screwed on there is only the barest margin, and no room at all for mistakes. It has to be done right . . . and that's when the strange music starts, when you stretch your luck so far that fear becomes exhilaration and vibrates along your arms. You can barely see at a hundred; the tears blow back so fast that they vaporize before they get to your ears. The only sounds are wind and a dull roar floating back from the mufflers. You watch the white line and try to lean with it . . . howling through a turn to the right, then to the left and down the long hill to Pacifica . . . letting off now, watching for cops, but only until the next dark stretch and another few seconds on the edge . . . The Edge . . . There is no honest way to explain it because the only people who really know where it is are the ones who have gone over. The others—the living—are those who pushed their control as far as they felt they could handle it, and then pulled back, or slowed down, or did whatever they had to when it came time to choose between Now and Later.*

Here we are beyond the ken of German existentialism. In Heidegger and Jaspers one finds no sense whatever for the poetry of such experiences. The philosopher who came closest to this kind of poetry was certainly Nietzsche.

It may be objected that he was a sickly recluse whose half-blind eyes barred him from such feats of daring; that he was in fact a very shy, if not a timid man; and that his talk of living dangerously was mere bluster. There is no denying that his health was so wretched that it was virtually nonexistent. But when the Franco-Prussian War broke out in 1870, Nietzsche, who was then a professor at Basel and hence a Swiss subject, volunteered and served at the front as a medical orderly. He was a shy man, but, unlike the German existentialists who never went anywhere, preferring the security of their university environment, Nietzsche was ever on the move and open to new perspectives. He was an experimentalist through and through: in his life, as a thinker, and as a writer. He was always willing to try something new, while most professors prefer to play it safe. Style is no small matter, and a scholastic style is a sure sign of a lack of daring or imagination, usually both.

While Nietzsche would surely have understood and felt the poetry of the passage from *Hell's*

---

* Hunter S. Thompson. *Hell's Angels.* New York: Ballantine Books, 1967, pp. 343–45. (. . .) indicates omissions while . . . represents Thompson's own punctuation.

Angels, his own version of living dangerously was palpably different. Crude amateur psychologists whose conception of heroism has not advanced beyond childish melodrama may suppose that his version was only a substitute for real daring. Subtler psychologists—Nietzsche, to be specific, and Kierkegaard, too—noted that it is precisely the cyclist who is seeking to escape from something, from problems he cannot resolve—and that speed can be a drug.

The quotation from *Hell's Angels* continues: "But the edge is still Out there. Or maybe it's In. The association of motorcycles with LSD is no accident of publicity. They are both a means to an end, to the place of definition."

Unquestionably, the cyclists and those who try LSD seek life at the limits, live dangerously, at the edge—and sometimes fall over. But that is also true of many warriors and criminals. Courage is admirable but often sought and displayed in destructive ways that bring ruin to others. Nor is self-destruction unproblematic.

In his "Prologue" Nietzsche's Zarathustra proclaims: "I love those who do not know how to live, except by going under [by perishing], for they are those who cross over [the bridge to the overman]." Still, we should distinguish between those who burn themselves out like Nietzsche himself, Van Gogh, and Mozart, who gave all they had to the most intense creative effort, and those who destroy themselves wantonly by taking drugs or riding their bikes at record speeds.

At first glance the great poets who wrote of their own despair or celebrated the beauty of the most intense suffering seem poles apart from the few who expressed a social conscience, writing about a brutalized toiler, the leaden-eyed, or the coal mines. But as soon as we compare them with youths who take drugs or lose control on an oil-slick and kill themselves and perhaps others as well, Shakespeare and Mozart appear in a different light. Few men have ever given such solace to so many who needed it.

21

If some readers would associate the passage from *Hell's Angels* with existentialism, that is surely due not to Jaspers and Heidegger but to French existentialism. Sartre and Camus have popularized that side of Nietzsche, which the German professors ignored along with Nietzsche's psychology. It may seem to be an *ad hominem* argument that is impermissible, but it is no argument whatever but simply a symptomatic fact; Camus's very poor health and Sartre's being wall-eyed did not keep these two men from taking great risks when the Nazis occupied France. Their most influential writings were the fruit of these formative experiences. That does not exempt their works from criticism. On the contrary, Camus's books may well have been overrated for a long time, in part because he had exceptional charm and had shown great courage. What matters here is that his work, as well as Sartre's, was born of firsthand experiences of life at the limits. These men did not write plays and novels about extreme situations because they had read Jaspers and Heidegger, but because they had seen the collapse of established ways of life and because they themselves had lived, and their friends had lived, dangerously. Yet when they tried to philosophize they came to grief.

Camus, who had no head for philosophy and no adequate training either, became portentous. Sartre never developed a philosophical style of his own but aped the worst kind of professorial German. The lucidity of his plays and novels offers an almost incredible contrast to the turgid opacity of his philosophical works. Nor could either of the two men resist the temptation to liven up their essays by often saying silly things that might appear startling. At such points they seem to be in a café or at a cocktail party, making remarks not worthy of being preserved in print, the more so because they quite lacked the wit of, say, Shaw, or Nietzsche's poetic power.

For all their faults, these men made millions of people in many countries aware of life at the limits as a subject that should concern philosophers and thoughtful people. Some had learned this earlier from Kierkegaard or Nietzsche; far more learned it from these two French writers who also went beyond their predecessors by associating life at the limits with a social conscience.

Their nineteenth-century predecessors had been preoccupied with themselves and with others who were more or less like them—with exceptional human beings, not with the masses. Indeed, both Nietzsche and Kierkegaard had such an extreme contempt for conformism that they also despised "the crowd," "the mob." For Sartre and Camus, on the other hand, the oppressed and the hungry loomed almost as large as Christ did for Kierkegaard. Neither of the two French writers ever arrived at any well-reasoned position on the relation of art and philosophy to starvation and misery. When Sartre did not feel like writing philosophy, he claimed that one could not write it while children were starving, but then he proceeded to write a vast multi-volume critical study on a French novelist, Gustave Flaubert. Still, he changed the sensibilty of a whole generation, not only in his own country.

The vast international impact of Sartre and Camus is inseparable from the fact that much of their writing was plainly literature and not philosophy. Indeed, Camus could hardly be called a philosopher at all. Most of the greatest philosophers were not mere philosophers. Aristotle was a scientist as well; Descartes and Leibniz were mathematicians of genius; Hume and Hegel were in their different ways also historians; Hobbes translated Homer as well as Thucydides; Spinoza wrote a Hebrew grammar and pioneered Bible criticism; Kant advanced a major astronomical theory. But the only major philosophers who greatly increased our understanding of life at the limits bridge philosophy and literature: Kierkegaard, Nietzsche, and Sartre. Not one of the great philosophers was an artist.

IV

WESTERN ART

22

Any attempt to understand life at the limits in terms of twenty-four categories is rather like trying to paint a sunset, using twenty-four colors. This can be brought off by mixing the colors and by realizing that the colors in the finished picture defy any simple identification—and the colors in the sky even much more so.

The people who developed the English language were more interested in making distinctions between boats than they were in the differences between colors or feelings, not to speak of tastes and smells. It is astonishing how few words we have for experiences of that kind and how many for seaworthy craft. The situation is essentially the same in other languages, except that the Arabs, for example, are less interested in boats than in camels.

One could try to remedy this situation by developing an intricate vocabulary for life at the limits. But as we consider the visual arts it should become clear that the use of two hundred categories would not greatly improve our understanding of life at the limits and the human condition. There was a point to showing how life at the limits involves much more than death, dread, and despair, but the multiplication of categories yields diminishing returns and is even likely to obstruct our understanding of what matters. The best way to understand the paintings of Michelangelo, Rembrandt, or Turner is hardly to count the colors in them with the help of a highly sophisticated color vocabulary.

In this chapter we shall concentrate on sculpture, painting, and graphic art. Photography and film will be considered very briefly, but applied arts and architecture will be ignored because they are less relevant to our themes. Nor shall we deal with the dance, for we lack information about it in former times when it was more important in the Western world, and in modern times it has become a marginal art form in the West. In any case, it would be folly to aim at completeness, and the approach will be highly selective. Many indubitably very great artists will be left out altogether because it makes more sense to try to learn something from a few artists.

23

Much of ancient Egyptian and Near Eastern art is a bold response to death, an act of defiance, a bid for a triumph over decay and oblivion. It was a keen sense of the limits of life that prompted most of this art.

What had happened once and was gone in a moment, more quickly than clouds change their shapes, was captured in stone. Sometimes faces that time would change even before death and decomposition would destroy them utterly were recreated in granite and limestone to survive the whole civilization, and some were far older in Jesus' time than he would be today. Their beauty, their character, and the way they looked are still known to us.

Some portraits record determination, suffering, and courage; some of the subjects had tasted despair and prevailed. But they are exceptions. In the first half of the third millennium the fourth dynasty in Egypt produced some heads of this sort. A somewhat later bronze head of a man, found at Nineveh, probably a portrait of King Sargon of Akkad, comes to mind in this connection. It is now in Baghdad Museum, and two color plates of it are included in André Parrot's *Sumer* (1961).

From the first half of the second millennium two individuals confront us. There is a head of Hammurabi in greenish blue steatite, now in the Louvre. Parrot, who reproduces it in black and white, comments: ". . . the sculptor has carved the worn, emaciated features, on which perhaps illness has left its mark, of a Hammurabi well advanced in years."

In Egypt the features of a slightly earlier king are far better known to us. Many major Egyptian museums have portrait heads of a pharaoh whom one instantly recognizes because his face is so distinctive: Sesostris III. He looks like a man without illusions who had an exceptionally keen sense of human frailty, suffering, and death. One description of the so-called Carnarvon head of Sesostris in the Metropolitan Museum of Art in New York remarks that "the expression of the mouth seems melancholy rather than disdainful. The head, for all its fleshlike quality, is carved in one of the hardest stones used by the Egyptians," quartzite. Other versions, including a full-length statue in the British Museum, were done in granite. The choice of stone seems more felicitous than adjectives like "melancholy" or "disdainful." What we see is total disillusionment and strength enough to live with it. Sesostris clearly knew what Sartre said in *The Flies:* "Life begins on the other side of despair."

This man of the nineteenth century B.C., who lived long before Moses and much more than a thousand years before the Buddha, Confucius, Lao-tze, or the first stirrings of Greek philosophy, we know from his portraits as if death had never come to him. It is not until fully five hundred years after his time that we again encounter historical figures whose visual images are as alive as that: men and women of the Amarna period in Egypt, most notably Akhenaton, his mother Tiye, and his wife Nefertiti. The painted limestone head of Nefertiti in West Berlin is as famous as any sculptured head anywhere but is widely admired more for its marvelous preservation, its pleasing bright colors, and the queen's beauty than for her expression, which hardly anyone seems to notice. Her expression is rather subtle and easier to read if one has also seen a not nearly so famous unpainted head of Nefertiti in Cairo. The secret of her beauty is that there is nothing bland about it. She is no pretty young thing; hers is an unsheltered spirit that masters grief with pride and fortitude.

Perhaps there is no person before Rembrandt of whom we possess as many different portraits as of Akhenaton, and many of them have a spiritual quality. He has been called the first individual in world history and the first monotheist, and while both claims are dubious, some of his portraits capture the intensity of a quest that led beyond the boundaries of established religion and art to explore new forms. Here was a ruler who refused to be bound by precedent, who spurned security, and who boldly lived at the edge.

As incredible as any head of this unparalleled period and indeed of any time is an inlaid and painted ebony head, only four inches high and less than three in width, of Queen Tiye, the king's mother. It is illustrated in this book. These Egyptian sculptors and the men and women they portrayed knew life at the limits.

24

When one considers Greek art against this historical background one can hardly help being struck by the lack of any concern with life at the limits during both the archaic and the classical period. It is only because most people, including art historians, are more familiar with Greek art and knew it long before they ever discovered Egypt and Mesopotamia that this contrast is not a commonplace. In the Western world Greek art was the norm for so long that the typical first response to Egyptian art was rather patronizing: it was supposed to be repetitive, stiff, and stylized, and Egyptian sculptors and painters allegedly did not yet know how to do this or that. The Berlin Nefertiti was a sensation largely because it was so patently different from all that was usually said and believed about Egyptian art; it was so lifelike and perhaps even beat the Greeks at their own game—nine hundred years before Phidias and the Parthenon.

Phidias was not the quintessence of perfection. Indeed, most classical Greek art is too bland to be on a par with the masterpieces of the Greek archaic period, which ended roughly with the Persian destruction of the Acropolis in 480 B.C. The archaic sculptures in the little museum on the Acropolis are superb, but one still does not find in them an insistent probing of life at the edge.

The more one reflects on Greek art, the clearer it seems that Nietzsche's concept of the Apollinian is really helpful at this point. What he himself did with his contrast of the Apollinian and the Dionysian is open to criticism, and the ways in which many others have used it again and again in various contexts hardly merits consideration. Greek architecture and sculpture are Apollinian in the sense that they are content to stay within drastic limits and try to achieve harmonious perfection, a triumph of proportion, not of defiant will.

For a long time the temples and sculptures inspired absurd misconceptions of ancient Greek culture, down to Matthew Arnold's "sweetness and light." How could such a view have been widely shared in the face of Greek tragedy? From the *Iliad* and *Agamemnon* to *The Bacchae,* the last play of Euripides, much of the finest Greek literature makes this notion ridiculous. Nietzsche associated the dark side of Hellenic culture and the will to exceed all limits with Dionysus and then understood Greek tragedy as a synthesis of the Dionysian and Apollinian. For the tragic poets also worked within very drastic limits. The longest extant tragedy has less than eighteen hundred lines, and no tragic poet worked with more than three actors, though some of the actors played more than one role. Still, the tragic poets explored life at the limits, while the sculptors and painters did not.

It is only in its last phase, after the death of Greek tragedy, that Greek sculpture changed. When Alexander the Great conquered the Persian Empire, including Egypt as well as Mesopotamia, Greek art ceased to be Greek and became "Hellenistic." In form, Hellenistic art is far closer to Greek art than it is to Egyptian or Mesopotamian art, but the spirit is no longer Apollinian. Suddenly Greek art acquires "soul" and becomes somewhat expressionistic. The Hellenistic sculpture that is best known shows this at a glance: Laokoon with his two sons, wrestling two huge serpents that are trying to crush them. It is illustrated in this book. For centuries this was considered the greatest creation of Greek art. Now it is sometimes said that the melodramatic pose cannot conceal a lack of passion. A subtle taste may well find more life and intensity in the tiny ebony head of Queen Tiye and more energy in a battered portrait of Sesostris than in this huge marble group. The fact remains that the famous Laokoon differs from classical and archaic Greek art by trying to show us life at the limits and transfigured terror.

The faces of Alkyoneus and his mother Gaia, the Earth, in the Pergamon Altar in East Berlin invite comparison with Laokoon's and illustrate the same theme. Other famous examples include the "Dying Persian" in the Terme Museum (illustrated in this book), the "Dying Gaul" in the Capitoline Museum, and the "Gaul Killing Himself and His Wife" in the Terme Museum —all in Rome.

In a very different way, more akin to the explosion of boundaries in the last movement of Beethoven's Ninth Symphony, the Winged Nike from Samothrace, in the Louvre, is anti-Apollinian and a far cry from archaic and classical Greek art. It represents a revolt against the medium, an attempt to transcend the limits of life on earth, and succeeds as a woman's huge marble body takes wing and appears to soar.

The Nike invites comparison with the archaic Zeus Carrying Off Ganymede, in Olympia. The story had it that Ganymede was carried off to Zeus' abode in the heavens or on Mount Olympus, but in the sculpture there is no sense of transcending terrestrial limits or of approaching them; what we are shown is a man walking fast as he carries a boy in his right arm.

Perhaps the work of Greek, as opposed to Hellenistic, art that comes closest to a sense of life at the limits is the head of a horse that may well be Phidias' masterpiece. The head is at the far right of the east pediment of the Parthenon and has long been in the British Museum along with the other Elgin Marbles. The horse, pulling the quadriga of the moon goddess, is about to "go under" the sea as the moon sets.

This Greek marble horse may be considered a member of a trinity. Two other ancient animal sculptures bring to mind life at the limits no less poignantly. The first is a bull's head done in copper in Sumer during the first half of the third millennium. It is now in the City Art Museum in St. Louis, and there is an excellent color photograph of it in Parrot's Sumer. The other sculpture stands in the Palazzo dei Conservatori in Rome and was done by an Etruscan sculptor in the early fifth century B.C. This bronze she-wolf has more soul than any Roman sculpture of a man or woman. The boys she is nursing, Romulus and Remus, are altogether different in style. They were made in the fifteenth century to replace babies destroyed by lightning in 65 B.C., and they are, in one word, *kitsch*. But the expression of the mother brings to mind danger, death, and devotion.

It is widely believed that camp or *kitsch* is a distinctively modern phenomenon. Actually, the Italian baroque is full of it—the Certosa di Pavia and the Isola Bella furnish some extreme examples—nor did it first emerge in the Renaissance. It abounded in Italy even in antiquity, and initially it flourished precisely where one might least expect to find it, in Etruscan funerary sculpture. Those who know the heights reached by Etruscan art long before the Romans could point to anything comparable might suppose that the Etruscans, unlike the Romans, had a sure sense of style. And one might assume further that camp in the face of death was a creation of twentieth-century undertakers. Yet it was precisely when faced with the limits of life that Etruscan art became grotesque. The sculptures of the deceased that they placed on their sarcophagi were occasionally high art but more often *kitsch*. (See illustrations of both types.)

The Romans could do idealized as well as very naturalistic portraits, but many of their sculptures were simply ridiculous. The reasons for the unintended bizarreness of much of their art are not always the same, but in the imperial age one frequent source of grotesque effects was gigantism. A huge head of the Emperor Constantine who made Christianity the state religion of the Empire is a fair example. (Some scholars consider it a portrait of his successor, Constantius II.) The camera case, included in the picture to give some idea of the scale, measures about half a foot (16 centimeters).

Eventually Christianity went far beyond the funerary *kitsch* of the Etruscans. No reaction to life at the limits that we know from antiquity equals the camp we encounter in the Capuchin Catacombs in Rome and Palermo. (See illustrations.)

The attitude of these Italian monks toward the dead offers a striking contrast to the austerity of the ancient Egyptians and is not dreamed of in existentialism. One might suppose that the monks do not see these corpses as we do, but while the pictures shown here are the author's, the picture postcards available at the catacombs are not essentially different.

25

One might suppose that the concern with distress and death, with life at the limits and attempts to transcend the limits, must have been a distinctive feature of Christian art from the beginning. The facts are otherwise. For more than a thousand years these themes, so prominent in Hellenistic art, were abandoned. They did not appear again until the Gothic period, after the Crusaders had returned to the Near East.

The Christ of early Christian and Romanesque art was not the Suffering Servant of Isaiah 53; he was the Lord. The cross was not seen as an instrument of torture before the high Middle Ages, and it was only then that the torments of the damned began to capture the imagination of sculptors. Why this sudden concern with anguish? It was clearly not derived straight from the Gospels, seeing that it emerged only after the Crusades had begun and then became much more pronounced in the fourteenth century.

Something must have happened then to lead people to associate Christianity with suffering and death, torture and anguish. The Crusades were undertaken in the name of Christianity and had this effect. Not only did the Crusaders themselves experience a great deal of misery, but the First Crusade began with a pogrom in the towns along the Rhine River in which, as Ernest Barker put it in the *Encyclopaedia Britannica* (eleventh edition), "10,000 Jews perished as first-fruits of crusading zeal." Three years later, in 1099, the Christians captured Jerusalem and burned the Jews of Jerusalem alive in their largest synagogue. An eyewitness of the capture, Raymond, gave an exultant account of what he saw:

> Wonderful sights were to be seen. Some of our men (and this was more merciful) cut off the heads of their enemies; . . . others tortured them longer by casting them into the flames. Piles of heads, hands, and feet were to be seen in the streets of the city. . . . Men rode in blood up to their knees and bridle reins. Indeed, it was a just and splendid judgment of God that this place should be filled with the blood of the unbelievers since it had suffered so long from their blasphemies.*

In 1204 the Crusaders sacked Constantinople, then still the capital of the Eastern Roman Empire and of Eastern Christendom, and destroyed countless ancient manuscripts and works of art, but some ancient art was carried off to the West, including the celebrated Greek bronze horses that adorn St. Mark's in Venice. Four years later Pope Innocent III called for a crusade to exterminate the Albigensians, who were peaceable heretics in southern France. In 1209 the Crusaders conquered the town of Béziers and exterminated every man, woman, and child in it, including those who were not heretics. The papal legate wrote the pope that the Crusaders had made "a huge slaughter, pillaged and burned the whole city, by reason of God's wrath wondrously kindled against it." When they took the castle of Bram, the Crusaders plucked out the eyes of more than a hundred victims and also cut off their noses. In 1215, when the Magna Carta was signed in England, Pope Innocent convened the Fourth Lateran Council which proclaimed that "Catholics who assume the cross and devote themselves to the extermination of heretics shall

---

* In August C. Krey. *The First Crusade: The Accounts of Eye-Witnesses and Participants.* Princeton, Princeton University Press, 1921, p. 261.

enjoy the same indulgence and privilege as those who go to the Holy Land." The other decrees of this church council in effect created the Inquisition, and in 1231 Pope Gregory IX burned a group of heretics in Rome. His successor, Innocent IV, issued a papal bull that officially authorized torture in cases of heresy. This is the context in which the concern with suffering and death, anguish and torture emerged in Christian art.

At the very least initially, the portrayals of the torments of the damned were part of the terror and meant to frighten people. One was not meant to feel any compassion, much less admiration for noble failures.

In the fourteenth century the portrayals of misery became still more prominent, and one often finds faces that express poignant grief. The Black Death ravaged Europe from 1347 until 1351, killing approximately one-third of the whole population. In stone and wood, sculptors immortalized faces they had seen.

26

Humanism is in its primary sense a syndrome that distinguished the Renaissance. It signifies the rediscovery of classical antiquity and a renewed respect for humanity as well as humane attitudes. All this does not entail any special concern with boundary situations, and many Renaissance artists lacked that. But at the height of the Renaissance, between 1470 and 1570, four artists consummated this theme in remarkably different ways that could not be surpassed.

Matthias Grünewald did this as a painter, notably in his Isenheim Altar pieces, now in Colmar in Alsace. His transcendence of the Gothic style helped to inspire modern expressionism. At the same time Hieronymus Bosch created paintings crowded with torments, in a new style that anticipated modern surrealism.

A little later, toward the end of this unprecedented period, Pieter Bruegel, who knew Bosch's work, placed human beings, whose endless follies and cruelties he recorded relentlessly but to all appearances without any passion, in nature, which no Western artist had done before him. For his predecessors, including even Leonardo da Vinci, nature had been at most an enchanting background. In Bruegel's paintings nature is the world we live in and is quite as indifferent to human suffering as most men are.

There is nothing melodramatic or sentimental in Bruegel's work. Whether he paints "The Triumph of Death," "The Suicide of Saul," or "The Procession to Calvary," cripples or a group of blind men, the style is never far different from his painting of "Children's Games," and there are people who associate him mainly with his "Peasants Dancing" and "The Peasants' Wedding," thinking of him as a cheerful sort.

"The Procession to Calvary" is as rich as reality looks to an artist. One simply cannot see it all at a glance; one feels impelled to break it up by focusing on details, as editors of illustrated books about Bruegel do. Yet the painting is not a composite work in which pictures of this group and that have been pieced together. It is a world in which an artist might wander around with his sketchbook or camera, finding countless scenes that could be framed in any number of ways. The human realities here are as crowded and varied as in a city in India, and an art historian has counted more than five hundred people on this one canvas. A crowd arranged in a circle around two crosses is waiting in the distant background on the right, and there is room for one more cross to be put up in the center. Elsewhere men are hanging from gallows, and crows abound, waiting, it seems, to peck out the eyes of the dead. Many people, including children, are on their way to witness the crucifixions, and the artist portrays, once again, children's games. In the center Jesus has just collapsed under the weight of the cross he is carrying, but the world little notes his suffering, and if the picture makes one central point, this is it. On the left some soldiers are trying to compel Simon of Cyrene to come with them in order to help Jesus carry the cross, but he resists them with all his strength and is helped by his wife, a sturdy fighter with a fierce expression—and a rosary with a cross dangling from her waist. Bruegel never raises his voice, and it is easy not even to notice such tiny details; yet the bold anachronism leaves no doubt about his feelings.

In his painting of Saul's suicide one must search for Saul, as in Chinese paintings with titles like "Fishing on a Wintry River" or "Asking about the Tao in the Autumn Mountains" one has to look and keep looking to find the human figures. Again, the world is largely indifferent to the despair of even the most illustrious, and events that loom large in literature later on attract no attention whatever when they happen. Even the few who realize this as they look at this picture are not at all likely to note the significance of the subject matter.

Saul is a profoundly tragic figure—more so than anyone else in the Bible—and his suicide is the epitome of nobility even in failure. Saul, who was "from his shoulders upward taller than any of the people" (I Samuel 9:2), brings to mind Ajax in the *Iliad*, who towered head and shoulders above all the other heroes (3.226 f.). Sophocles wrote a tragedy on Ajax' madness and suicide, and Saul's madness and suicide were also tragic. Yet—or rather, therefore—Christianity largely ignored his suicide, and Western literature discovered it only in the sixteenth century. In 1552 a Spaniard, Vasco Diaz Tanco, published *Tragedia de Amon y Saul*, which has not survived. Hans Sachs, in Germany, wrote *Tragedia Koenig Sauls*, and an unknown Italian wrote *La Rapresentatione della distruttione di Saul*—all in the 1550s. In medieval Christian art representations of Saul were confined almost entirely to illuminated manuscripts, and even there the scenes illustrated were how Samuel anointed him, how David played the harp before him, and how he found David in a cave. It remained for Bruegel in 1562 to paint Saul's suicide.

Bruegel's concern with life at the limits has been widely ignored along with his distinctive experience of life. For much of the nineteenth century Raphael was the perfect painter, and when popular taste embraced Bruegel in the twentieth century, it was because he was felt to have been amusing. In fact, he was a highly original painter who in many ways represents a *non plus ultra*. His stature is not a function of one single point, but his art is also a triumph of compassion and a protest against callousness.

27

Grünewald, Bosch, and Bruegel were overshadowed by a contemporary whose *terribilità* stunned his own age and changed the course of Western art. The Italian word that came to be associated with him as soon as people saw his paintings on the ceiling of the Sistine Chapel shows how the element of terror in Michelangelo's art was felt from the beginning.

He was the heir of the Hellenistic sculptors whose virtuosity he equaled, and in sculpture after him hollow, bombastic visual rhetoric flourished. Once again one could make marble do practically anything, and one did, as technique triumphed over spirit, and melodrama and sentimentality over feeling, in painting as well as sculpture. But Michelangelo's genius can be distinguished from his superlative skill, which was approximated by others and merely speeded developments that were well on their way.

Michelangelo made the Sistine Chapel the greatest single monument of Western painting by his visual recreation of the spirit of the Hebrew Bible. He made available to all who could see the sublimity of the creation story in Genesis. He showed all who raised their eyes to behold his frescoes the awesomeness of this ancient conception of God and man, surrounding the central scenes with overpowering prophets and sibyls whom he depicted in extreme states—none more so than Jonah, whom he placed above the altar, defying God.

Many decades later, Michelangelo returned to the Sistine Chapel to paint the wall over the altar—under Jonah. He did a Last Judgment, dealing nakedly with life at the limits and including vast suffering. But Jesus as judge of all in the center is, though closer to us, dwarfed by Jonah, and so is the misery of all who suffer under his curse.

A letter Michelangelo wrote to Giovanfrancesco Fattucci in Rome, at the end of December 1523, is very forthright. The pope had wanted him to paint twelve apostles when he did the ceiling, but it seemed to Michelangelo that the plan would turn out wretchedly, and he so informed the pope. "He asked me why; I told him, because they were also wretched." *Perchè furon poveri anche loro.* For Michelangelo the Hebrew prophets and the pagan sibyls were beings of a higher order than Jesus' apostles, who were to his mind totally unsuitable for his attempt to create a new image of man—or to resuscitate the unsurpassed grandeur of the Old Testament.

Although Michelangelo thought of himself as primarily a sculptor, he was denied the opportunity to create in stone a monument even remotely comparable to what he achieved in paint in the Sistina. He thought of the tomb of Pope Julius II along these lines, but what he was finally permitted to do was on a far smaller scale. The monument is dominated totally by a marble Moses, whose striking similarity to God in Michelangelo's version of the creation of sun and moon seems to have gone largely unnoticed. Like the prophets and sibyls, this Moses is no wretch.

The slaves that the sculptor carved for the same monument carry his concern with the limits further. Some are in the Louvre now, more in the Academy in Florence. Here technique is wholly harnessed by spirit, and even the finished pieces look like incarnate extreme conditions, while the unfinished slaves break altogether new ground as they struggle to emerge from stone and their efforts are plainly hopeless. These sculptures in Florence are uncanny symbols of man's plight.

Michelangelo's deep concern with distress and despair finds expression in a quatrain he wrote. An admirer had said in a short poem that the artist's marble "Night" was so lifelike that one needed only to speak to her and she would wake up. The sculptor had his statue reply (in John Addington Symonds' translation):

> Sweet is my sleep, but more to be mere stone,
> So long as ruin and dishonour reign;
> To hear nought, to feel nought, is my great gain:
> Then wake me not, speak in an under-tone.

Visually, his concern with suffering gains its most moving expression in his late pietàs, which are utterly different from the more famous youthful one in St. Peter's in Rome. There we see an eternally youthful beautiful young Adonis or Osiris lying in the lap of his equally youthful and beautiful sister-wife, and all is loveliness. There is nothing Biblical about the celebrated pietà in Rome. The Gospels do not mention that Mary ever cradled her crucified son's corpse, and this is not a body that could have just been taken down from a cross. The motif is not Biblical but comes from the pre-Christian Near East.

The late pietàs breathe an altogether different spirit. Here the corpse is that of the Suffering Servant, and in the version in the cathedral of Florence, Nicodemus, looking down upon death and despair, bears the features of the sculptor himself. What one might have thought was too terrible to look at has been transfigured by art.

28
Rembrandt*

> Deep crimson velvet lined with ermine fur,
> pictures of women's breasts and eager thighs
> seem dull and dead before the sunken eyes
> of my creations: beggars whom you slur,
>
> the poor, the old, the Jews—the scum that crowds
> into the fringes of your wealthy towns:
> Without the benefit of purple gowns,
> or naked bodies under silken shrouds,
>
> without a multicolored interplay,
> I model them out of the dark of night,
> bring them to life with but a beam of light,
> as God created us from dirt and clay.
>
> The mud-brown portrait of some beggar sage,
> a little etching, all restraint and quiet,
> contains more life than all the Baroque riot
> and infinite contortions of this age.

Rembrandt found beauty where others had not seen it. He painted those who lived at the edge—sometimes as Biblical characters but, whether he did that or not, always as people who had depth and dignity. In the interplay of a little light with much darkness he found enchantment. Like no man before him, he kept painting his own face, and as he aged and became, according to common sense, less and less pleasant to look at, his self-portraits became more haunting and more beautiful.

Earlier artists had sometimes found ways of including self-images in large works. Dürer, who did this in a few paintings, also painted three outright self-portraits that are as famous as they are beautiful—the last of them dated 1500, when he was twenty-nine. What Rembrandt did involved a new way of seeing oneself, of seeing the process of aging, of seeing humanity abandoned to time and decay.

No other artist has done so much to change our view of life at the limits. Goya called Rembrandt his master. Clearly, my own way of seeing humanity owes more to Rembrandt than to anyone else.

* From *Cain*.

29

The sculptures of the High Renaissance bring to mind those of the Hellenistic period, which ushered in an age of decline. Anyone much impressed by parallels between different cultures might therefore have predicted that after Michelangelo European art could scarcely help going the same way, and in sculpture it did to some extent. At his best, Bernini was still a fine sculptor in the Hellenistic manner, but much of the Baroque and what came after was painfully melodramatic; the pathos was often utterly hollow; and the modern term "camp" fits a great deal of this art. Once again one was able to do realistic portraits or to idealize them at will. But for roughly three hundred years European sculpture was in eclipse. Some would grant that Rodin was a great sculptor; others may feel that some later sculptor—Epstein perhaps or Henry Moore— marks a new beginning, but we may be too close to all these to be sure, and it is not impossible that sculpture has declined again as it did at the end of antiquity.

What is clearly different this time is that art found another medium, painting, in which new worlds were conquered. The ancient world produced many fine frescoes, notably in Egyptian and Etruscan tombs, but after the Hellenistic age painting also declined. There were no painters then remotely comparable to Bosch and Bruegel or Michelangelo and Rembrandt. Yet one may wonder whether after Rembrandt European painting had any place left to go. For at least two hundred years after Rembrandt's death there was scarcely another European painter of the same stature as those just considered here.

Of course, there is no lack of famous names during the two centuries following Rembrandt's death in 1669, precisely one hundred years after Bruegel's death. Vermeer outlived Rembrandt by a few years. But the great artists of the eighteenth and early nineteenth centuries represent a marked decline in originality, except for two astonishing painters who came close to concealing their genius from their contemporaries.

30

Goya was born in 1746, three years before Goethe, and died in 1828, four years before Goethe, and like Goethe he was outwardly a pillar of the establishment, immensely successful, widely appreciated, and he worked to the very end of his long life. He was an extraordinarily gifted painter who could do portraits of the people at the Spanish court that pleased the subjects but are often profound. Yet if he had died at forty-five—an age that Van Gogh and Toulouse-Lautrec, Mozart Schubert, Byron and Shelley never even approximated—one would have no reason to consider him one of the most remarkable artists of all time.

A severe illness in 1792 left him permanently deaf. After that his art took a new turn, although he never ceased to paint masterly portraits. On January 4, 1794, Goya sent Don Bernardo de Iriarte, the Vice-Protector of the Academy, "a set of cabinet pictures in which I have managed to make observations for which there is normally no opportunity in commissioned works, which give no scope for fantasy and invention." Several of these pictures represent scenes from a bullfight, one shows "Brigands Attacking a Coach," another "The Shipwreck or the Flood." "The Fire at Night" shows a group of people struggling in the foreground and a sky with colors not found anywhere in art before Turner. Still more revealing is a painting Goya himself described in a second letter, January 7: ". . . it represents a yard with lunatics and two of them fighting completely naked while their warder beats them, and others in sacks; (it is a scene I saw in Saragossa)." This painting [330], now in the Meadows Museum in Dallas, is reproduced in color in *The Life and Complete Work of Francisco Goya with a catalogue raisonné of the paintings, drawings, and engravings*, with 2148 illustrations.*

It has been suggested that Goya may have known Hogarth's madhouse scene in the last of the eight plates of "Rake's Progress," published sixty years earlier. Hogarth was above all a satirist who used engravings to bring to a large public scenes reminiscent of details in Bruegel's paintings and, rather more so, of the paintings of Adriaen van Ostade and Jan Steen, seventeenth-century masters who provide a clear link between Bruegel and Hogarth. Ostade and Steen are often funny, and their humor is scarcely black. They are dealing not with the limits of life but sometimes with the lower strata of society and with petty crime. Their paintings are usually very agreeable, cozy, and seem intended to make us smile. Hogarth is a moralist and often sarcastic, and the crudity of the moral of "Rake's Progress"—behold, he ends in a madhouse—is relieved by the fact that

---

* For the letters and small black-and-white pictures of the other paintings, see pp. 108–12 and 169. Numbers in square brackets after pictures mentioned in the text above refer to the catalogue raisonné.

the antics of some of the inmates are likely to make us laugh. But Goya's *Corral de locos* [330] is terrifying, like much of his later work, and it has a symbolic dimension. Indeed, this painting could have been entitled *La condition humaine*. As the two men fight and the warder beats them, a lunatic in the background raises his arms like a priest; one in the foreground roars; another, seated, grins; and yet another, on the floor, seems to egg them on but looks like a snarling dog.

In Goya's paintings the sufferings and madness of humanity erupt only now and then with frightful force; for example, in "The Spell" [661]. From his graphic work we know that the French invasion of Spain and the brutalities of the war moved life at the limits into the center of Goya's vision. But of the paintings that show this, few are widely known, and only "The Third of May 1808" [984] is as famous as his many portraits of this period. Yet an 1812 inventory listed "twelve [paintings] of the Horrors of the War," and there are many other paintings that have similar subjects, including "Savages Murdering a Woman," prison scenes, "Monks Throwing Books and Papers on the Fire," "Heap of Corpses," "Village on Fire," and "The Hurricane" [914–50]. Sometime between 1812 and 1819 Goya also painted "The Madhouse" [968] and several pictures dealing with the Inquisition, flagellants, and exorcism [966–79]. Yet few even of those who greatly admire Goya are aware of these paintings. Goya is widely known for his magnificent portraits and his etchings. And hearing him linked with life at the limits, most people would think of one series of etchings in particular, *The Disasters of War*.

Goya's last paintings are quite as remarkable as his graphic work. After another serious illness in 1819, he decorated his home, known as *La Quinta del Sordo* (The deaf man's house) with fourteen "black paintings" now in the Prado in Madrid [1615–27a]. Few men have ever attempted such large and powerful works in their seventies. One feels like saying that these pictures overwhelm the viewer who is compelled to share the artist's frightening visions. In fact, Goya's contemporaries did not know these works, and even some people who discuss them in print fail to understand them. There is a color reproduction of "Duel with Cudgels" [1616, large black-and-white photograph on page 320] in Abbruzzese's *Goya*. Keizō Kanki also offers a two-page reproduction in very different and misleading colors and comments:

> My own explanation of this gloomy scene, in which two men fight ferociously knee-deep in mire, is that Goya was trying to give expression to the two conflicting personalities within himself: mindless Aragonese tradition warring with the enlightenment the artist acquired in middle life. If this is not a scene depicting the artist's inner turmoil, the painting may be thought of as expressing the two contradictory ways of life prevalent in Spain at the time (p. 104f.).

The authors of *The Life and Complete Work of Francisco Goya* do not seem to have understood the picture either, but at least their description will make Goya's meaning obvious to many readers. Or will it?

> The *Duel* [1616] would be a barbarous but straightforward fight with cudgels between two peasants if it were not for the nightmare suggestion that the combatants are sinking into quicksand as they bludgeon each other to death; and the *Dog* [1612], perhaps the strangest of all the scenes, produces its powerfully disturbing effect by leaving everything to the spectator's imagination, with no possible answer to the question of the artist's own intention. . . . A dog is sinking into the quicksand, only his head still visible, alive—how much longer?—in a totally base and abstract setting. Such a subject defies analysis and belongs to the irrational world of dream and hallucination (p. 318f).

Nightmare? Irrational? Hallucination? No possible answer to the question of Goya's intention? Are some people who write about art as illiterate as people writing philosophy often are ignorant of the visual arts? Have they never read or seen Samuel Beckett's *Endgame?* Do they not know the conclusion of Kafka's *Trial?* " 'Like a dog!' he said; it was as if the disgrace should survive him."

Assuming that the identification of quicksand is right in both cases, no "analysis" is required, and the name of the "Duel" in the inventory of 1828, "Two Provincials," seems as apt as a scholar's attempt, in 1867, to identify them "as cattle herdsmen from Galicia" seems irrelevant. The first chapter of *The Dhammapada*, one of the oldest and most venerable Buddhist scriptures, is more to the point: ". . . The world does not know that we must all come to an end here; but those who know it—their quarrels cease at once." We are all dying slowly, and the end is not far off, but many people bludgeon each other to death, unaware that they are sinking. In the eleventh chapter of *The Dhammapada* it is said that "A man who has learnt little, grows old like an ox; his flesh grows, but his knowledge does not grow." Goya suggests that a man who has learned little dies like a dog—and one who has learned much is at least aware of the fact that he is dying as helplessly as a dog.

His interpreters have preferred not to understand him. Many have drawn comfort from a late drawing in black chalk that shows an old man with white hair and a long beard, stooped, walking with two canes, and bears the legend *Aun aprendo*, "I am still learning" [1758].

To understand Goya one must study his drawings and etchings, which show an incredible interest in life at the limits. Leonardo and Michelangelo had been unsurpassed draftsmen, Dürer excelled as an engraver, and Rembrandt's drawings and etchings sometimes have a haunting quality that is almost on a par with his paintings, but for all these men their abundant graphic work was still subsidiary. Goya, on the other hand, did several series of etchings that went beyond anything ever achieved in any medium. His closest forerunner was Jacques Callot, who had died during the Thirty Years' War, in 1635, and devoted himself entirely to the graphic arts. Callot's last two series of etchings were *The Small Miseries of War* (1632) and *The Large Miseries of War* (1633). "A Court Martial" in the *Large Miseries* is very impressive and may be seen as a bridge from Bruegel to Goya. The plate is crowded with details, but in the center is a tree that dominates the scene with more than twenty hanged men and a priest on a ladder holding up a cross. The horror of it is chilling, and yet Goya went much further in his epic exploration of life at the limits.

His first series of etchings, *Caprichos* (eighty plates), was published in 1799. Later he did three more: *La Tauromaquia* (1816), *Los Desastres de la Guerra* (1863), and *Los Proverbios* (1864, also known as *Disparates*). Goya's large painting, almost nine feet high and more than thirteen feet wide, "The Third of May, 1808," belongs with "The Disasters of War," which were done between 1810 and 1823. It shows a row of heavily armed soldiers shooting a small group of defenseless civilians; one has his arms flung high, while some others already lie on the ground, blood-soaked. Edouard Manet's "The Execution of Maximilian" is clearly based on this painting which is a visual outcry that lends a voice to the victims. But "The Disasters" are not studies for paintings; they are a self-contained work in a medium that has the power to reach large numbers of people, while a canvas—especially in those days—could be expected to be seen by very few.

The etchings with their succinct captions have a cumulative impact: "With reason, or without"; "And they are wild beasts"; "Is this what you were born for?"; "Bury them and be silent"; "Why?"; "Nobody knows why"; "Truth is dead." These plates push the exploration of human derangement and degradation, distress and despair further than the visual arts had ever gone.

Is this still transfigured terror? Is the dreadful made beautiful? Reactions differ. Some would say that this is clearly not Goya's intent; that he wants to produce outrage, not admiration or pleasure; that he aims at social change and not at satisfaction. Many admire him on that account, but few will ever look at the eighty-odd etchings of "The Disasters of War," one after another, and persevere to the end unless they do find them beautiful.

It is debatable whether this new art form—a series of roughly eighty etchings—works well as propaganda. An etching is a very subtle medium, and a good one often needs to be read again and again like a difficult poem that must be lived with to be understood. One simply cannot absorb eighty in a row. It may be objected that if people live with the series this is far better and much more likely to change their hearts. But who will live with Goya's "Disasters"? Hardly those who love war. Of course, there are many who do not love war but consider it justified in certain circumstances. Will their minds be changed by Goya's series?

Few but other artists have ever had the patience to study and live with one or more of Goya's complete series. If one merely shares the spirit of the sarcastic captions, one has soon had enough. And if one does not, more and more in the same vein do not change one's outlook. The variety of the subject matter is not sufficient as long as the tone remains the same. Only those who delight in Goya's art persevere.

One of the *Caprichos* [43] includes a legend in Goya's own handwriting: "The sleep of reason produces monsters." This could mean: Do not let reason go to sleep! As a supreme artist, did Goya also say, unwittingly: The monsters are terrifying, but I have the power to transfigure them; are they not beautiful?

El sueño de la razón could also mean the dream of reason, and in *The Life and Complete*

Work of Francisco Goya the title is translated that way. But Goya's own manuscript commentary, now in the Prado, reads: "Imagination deserted by reason creates impossible, useless thoughts. United with reason, imagination is the mother of all art and the source of all its beauty" (*Complete Etchings*, p. 19).

His many pictures of witches have sometimes been cited as evidence of his superstition, but a preparatory drawing for *Capricho* 43 is accompanied by Goya's explanation: "The Author dreaming. His only intention is to banish harmful common beliefs and to perpetuate with this work of *caprichos* the sound testimony of truth (*The Life and Work*, p. 125).

"The Disasters of War," though intended for publication, were so radical that they were not published until 1863 (eighty plates; three more were added in subsequent editions). "The [22] Proverbs" appeared in 1864.

Some of his most terrifying drawings Goya never made into etchings, and they were discovered in his notebooks still later. His album "C" seems to contain sketches of the mid-twentieth century. Above one drawing he wrote: "Poor man in Asia who sets his head aflame until they give him something" (C 50). A whole series shows victims of the Inquisition with such captions as: "For being of Jewish ancestry" (C 88), "For wagging his tongue in a different way" (C 89), and "For discovering the motion of the earth" (C 94). Yet we have been told again and again that only the Nazis persecuted Jews for being of Jewish descent, and a celebrated existentialist wrote a big book, *The Origins of Totalitarianism* (1951), without as much as mentioning the Inquisition. Often we can learn more from great artists than from philosophers. Yet we should not suppose that genuine artists are generally prompted by a purpose; they are obsessed by their visions and share them with others when circumstances permit.

31

French impressionism began almost exactly two hundred years after Rembrandt's death. Goya's influence on Manet during the crucial 1860s needs to be stressed. "The Execution of Maximilian" is by no means the only one of his paintings that was clearly inspired by Goya—actually, there are four versions of Manet's "Execution"—in Boston, in Copenhagen, in London, and in Mannheim. "The Fifer" brings to mind Goya's painting of a boy in a red suit, and Manet's pictures of bullfights, of which "The Dead Toreador" in Washington is a good example, point in the same direction. Once one has noted so many parallels, one can hardly doubt that his famous nude, "Olympia," was also inspired in part by the celebrated "Maya, Nude." Taken as a whole, however, French impressionism was not centrally preoccupied with life at the limits. It was a movement that breathed new life into painting after a long period of decline during which only two great painters stood out as great revolutionaries, but its primary concern was not with extreme situations but with color.

Actually, the French did not create impressionism. The first great impressionist was an Englishman, Joseph Mallord William Turner (1775–1851). But this fact was not appreciated, although he was widely known in his lifetime. Turner could do many things well, and his greatest and most original canvases came to be widely known and admired only after he had been dead more than a hundred years.

Much more so than the French impressionists, he was a true visionary and a loner, one who could not find comfort in a congenial group of artists who saw things similarly. It may be relevant that when Turner was twenty-five, his mother was committed to a mental hospital. Four years later, in 1804, she died insane. But what matters is that, unlike the French impressionists, he was fascinated by extreme situations.

It is instructive to look through a book with color illustrations of his work, to pick out the most impressionistic paintings that are boldest and most revolutionary, and then to check their titles: "The Shipwreck" (1805), "The Fall of an Avalanche" (1810), "Snowstorm: Hannibal and His Army Crossing the Alps" (1812, the year when Napoleon's Grand Army was annihilated in the snows of Russia), "Interior at Petworth" (about 1835; this title is an exception, but the painting exults in chaos), "Fingal's Cave" (1832), "A Fire at Sea" (1834), "The Burning of the Houses of Parliament" (1835), "Norham Castle, Sunrise" (1835–40), "The 'Fighting Téméraire' Tugged to Her Last Berth to Be Broken Up" (1838), "The Slave-ship" (1839), "Stormy Sea" (1835–40), "Snowstorm" (1842), "The Evening of the Deluge" (1843), and "The Morning after the

Deluge" (1843). A very few of his most striking pictures do not have names that dramatic; for example, "Rain, Speed, and Steam—The Great Western Railway" (1844). But it is as clear as can be that Turner loved the breaking up of established forms. Some of the canvasses that appealed to his contemporaries are a bit melodramatic, but the masterpieces with the bold titles are not merely rhetorical, florid, or pompous. They project a new way of seeing light and color, and the second picture of 1843 mentioned above is actually called: "Light and Colour (Goethe's Theory): the Morning after the Deluge."

What is exciting about these paintings is not their subject matter which is merely the occasion for the dissolution of the stable forms of common sense that had been accepted by almost all traditional painters. Turner is Dionysian; he delights in the breakup and finds extraordinary and exhilarating beauty in shipwreck and avalanche, fires, snowstorms, and the morning after the deluge.

French impressionism represents something like a second Renaissance in painting. For centuries this art had not witnessed such an explosion of genius, such excitement, such an array of outstanding artists. In at least two ways impressionism was actually more revolutionary than Renaissance painting. It came much more suddenly, and it was not a rediscovery of ancient art, a reconquest of forgotten skills, but above all a new way of seeing and painting.

There are so many men and women of great talent in this movement that from a distance one is apt to see a rather undifferentiated mountain range. As one looks closely, however, one can distinguish a few peaks that are remarkably different from each other.

There is Renoir, for example, whose talent was second to none and perhaps, by the very highest standards, his undoing. He seems to have had the ability to paint perfect pictures without much trouble, and his work is so uniformly lovely and pleasing that it seems to lack depth, not to speak of any sense for life at the limits.

Cézanne's work is much more rugged, and at times one feels that he was engaged in something enormously difficult, as if he had tried to construct or reconstruct nature. Still, he also was not attracted to extreme situations.

Claude Monet was, like Cézanne, something of a loner, though not nearly so solitary as either Goya or Turner, and during an exceptionally long life (1840–1926) moved very far from his beginnings. In the end he had emancipated himself almost entirely from the Western tradition, and his many paintings of water lilies—we really ought to call them lotus—have an Oriental and specifically Taoist quality. Turner had got as far almost a century earlier, but one would never mistake a Monet for a Turner. For in Monet there is no relish in destruction and chaos, no Dionysian cry of joy, but an astonishing sense of peace.

A very different extreme was explored by Toulouse-Lautrec, who died in his thirties (1864–1901). Crippled, he had a sense of life at the limits. He painted harlots and did not try to make them look beautiful, but his paintings, which do not try to hide squalor and ugliness, are not only sensitive but also extremely well designed, colorful, and, in one word, beautiful.

32
Van Gogh

An awkward Dutchman
shipwrecked
among subtle Frenchmen
who could paint the very air
a peasant
unaccustomed to sit back
to contemplate a still life or a dancer
loath to determine what we might behold
had not convention
cut patterns for immediate apprehension
he had no mind to paint distilled impressions.

Nature
had veiled her charms from Michelangelo
and gave herself to Rembrandt in her sleep.
To him
she opened up her heart.

> Flowers
> a patch of colors
> for others
> showed him faces.
> Compared to his
> tormented trees
> most men are dead.
>
> His reds and yellows
> greens and blues
> are not sensations nor attempts to please
> but fires that consumed his mind
> and leap to lick at yours.

Vincent van Gogh lacked the facility that made it possible for Turner and for Goya to be highly respectable and successful while also expressing their distinctive visions on the side. Initially, his taste for the limits, or rather his compulsion to come to terms with them, was shaped by his social conscience. He lived among miners and painted dark, deliberately crude pictures of them. He was hampered by a lack of facility, but he also had no wish to paint pretty pictures, and there was nothing glib in him. When he discovered light and color a little later, he still did not try to do what the French impressionists did, and when none of his works found buyers he never chose to compromise.

His intensity can be suggested in some measure by a few figures. His early dark pictures, including the famous "Potato Eaters," were done in 1885. He discovered color and his own distinctive style in 1887, and when he found that his madness was incurable, he committed suicide in 1890. He created literally hundreds of the finest paintings in the world in four years.

Since he was unable to sell any of them, it proved possible eventually to bring together 150 paintings and 400 drawings in a single building. No other artist has a shrine like the Rijksmuseum Vincent van Gogh in Amsterdam where these paintings are on display in chronological sequence. The only comparison that comes to mind—and it is not at all close—is the Sistine Chapel. In the mid-1970s, a few years after the museum had opened, the crowds coming to see the Michelangelos and the van Goghs were very different. The Sistine Chapel was crammed with noisy travel groups that gathered around guides who often disregarded the ubiquitous signs, reinforced by periodical announcements over a public-address system, demanding silence. In the museum there was a pervasive air of reverence. Most of the viewers were under thirty, and nobody spoke except in hushed tones. Even if none of them should have thought of it in quite this way, they felt that they were in the presence of life at the limits. What they saw was the documentation of such a life.

The subject matter is wholly secondary, except for van Gogh's self-portraits, of which a few are in Amsterdam and more elsewhere. These provide a record that has only one parallel: Rembrandt. But we find the same poignancy in van Gogh's pictures of his own room. One hangs in the van Gogh Museum, another in Paris, a third in Chicago. These pictures do not try to make any point and are totally lacking in rhetoric. They were not meant to speak to us or convince us of anything, and yet they are as moving as Goya's "Disasters of War."

To see how Nietzsche burned himself out during those very same years, part of the time only a few miles east of where van Gogh was painting, though the two men were totally unaware of each other, one has to read the books he wrote in the 1880s. That takes a long time, and one is distracted by the subject matter, by difficult philosophical problems, and sometimes also by overblown rhetoric. In the Rijksmuseum van Gogh enough of the work hangs on the walls of a single vast room on the second floor so that one can see it in less than an hour before immersing oneself in this picture and that; one can see many at once; and one feels in the presence of this whole life at the limits.

33

As we move into the twentieth century, we are struck by such a flood of names that have some relevance to our theme that it would certainly make sense to conclude this account of Western art with van Gogh. Moreover, these pages have been highly selective; we have considered only a few of the very greatest artists; and it may therefore be asked whether any twentieth-century artist ranks with those mentioned so far. Many would say that Picasso does; fewer would press the claims of other painters, sculptors, and graphic artists. But then we also omitted

Leonardo, Titian, and Rubens because their focus was not on life at the limits. It would therefore be no slight to ignore Picasso and stop these reflections on Western art at this point. Yet it does seem worthwhile to ask in what directions the exploration of life at the limits has proceeded in our time. Can one discern some major tendencies?

Just before French impressionism was born, a new art was born: photography. The two events were not unrelated. One of the major demands made on painting and sculpture could now be addressed to photography, and the impressionists made the most of their new freedom. Or did they? If painters needed no longer to record what cameras could record, and if people, still lifes, and landscapes did not have to be portrayed as they looked to ordinary people, then it soon became plain that the impressionists had come nowhere near making the most of the artist's freedom. Experiment and the search for novelty became the order of the day, and boundaries were now so easy to cross that the act no longer involved much daring. In former ages, the courage to transcend hallowed limits had to be drawn as a rule from a shattering experience in which the artist stood at the edge of life and saw an abyss. After that the judgments of one's contemporaries mattered less. In the twentieth century this changed. It took quite as much, or as little, courage to work in traditional forms. The demand for novelty became a pervasive feature of civilization, except in philosophy. Everything changed all the time—in the marketplace more than anywhere else. "New" came to be confused more and more with "better"; "old" with "uninteresting."

In a way, then, modern art has proceeded in almost all directions, and it would serve no purpose to try to catalogue them. But one can also lump together the whole trend toward novelty for novelty's sake as one of the major directions of modern art and then look for others. American cars are presented in new styles every year, and most of the differences are wholly nonfunctional. Cosmetics and detergents, as well as other household goods, are also presented as desirable because they are new and allegedly different. Here, too, the novelty often consists in nothing but the packaging. Artists have to try to make a living, and the pressure upon them to succumb to this trend is enormous. Every artist trying to make a living knows this. Only the cultured consumer may resent this comparison between art and advertising. But it actually is no mere comparison. The artist who approaches a gallery or a dealer and the photographers who wish to sell their work are met with the dreadful query: What is new and different about your work? There are many thousands or even hundreds of thousands who are competing. What is novel about you?

Of course, there are many cases in which one cannot draw a sharp line between those who have something to say and those who do not. Both types may work in traditional forms, and both may deviate from previous conventions and do something experimental. The important distinction is not that between the more traditional and the more experimental artists; it is that between having something new to say and novelty for novelty's sake. In the course of experiments one may, however, come to see something differently, and then one cannot really say that an artist who did experiment for experiment's sake did not in the process discover something. It remains pertinent to ask *what* was discovered and what an artist has to say. Literary critics at one time made much of "the heresy of paraphrase," fudging the crucial difference between the idiotic belief that a paraphrase of a poem might be adequate and as good as the poem itself and the reasonable question what, if anything, a poet was saying. Nobody will suppose that one can adequately paraphrase a painting or a sculpture, an etching or a photograph. But there is no good reason for not asking what, if anything, the artist has seen that might affect our vision.

34

Picasso was one of the most gifted artists of all time. His facility, which is not generally appreciated in its full measure, is an indispensable clue to his career as an artist. Consider *Picasso: The Blue and Rose Periods: A Catalogue Raisonné of the Paintings, 1900–1906.* This volume merely spans the beginning of his career, from the ages of nineteen to twenty-five, and he kept working until he died in his nineties. For these early years alone the admittedly incomplete catalogue lists and illustrates 468 paintings that exhibit the most astonishing versatility. Rembrandt did not paint that many pictures during his whole life. Dürer, who was relatively prolific, left us less than two hundred paintings; Bruegel, Vermeer, and Leonardo less than fifty each.

As one studies these early Picassos one gets the sense that this young painter could do whatever he wished. A pastel of 1900 called "Entrance to the Bullring" shows how the nineteen-year-old could do what Matisse did later, and that the youth could do it better. An oil painting of the same year, "Le Moulin de la Galette," now in the Guggenheim Museum, shows that he could also paint like a major impressionist, although the colors anticipate Emil Nolde. "Bullfight," done the following year, transposes Goya into an impressionist painting, while the "Portrait of Pedro Mañach," also 1901, exceeds the austerity of Cézanne. And then, still the same year, Picasso found a style of his own, that of his so-called Blue Period. Some of the finest examples are in American museums: "The Tragedy" in the National Gallery in Washington, "The Old Guitarist" in Chicago, and "La Vie" in Cleveland, to cite only three pictures of 1903 that poignantly portray life at the limits.

It would be easy to lengthen the list, for the central theme of the Blue Period is the beauty of despair. But Picasso seems to have found very quickly that he had solved that problem in blue and that it was pointless to repeat over and over what he had done so well. By 1904 he tried to do something similar in shades of gray, in "The Woman Ironing," which is now in the Guggenheim Museum in New York, and then, using shades of pink, in "Woman with a Crow," now in Toledo, Ohio. Having solved that problem also, Picasso began to explore life at the limits in another sense, with a large series of paintings of the life of acrobats. He may not have known that Nietzsche had developed this metaphor for life at the edge in the Prologue to his *Zarathustra*, and he could not possibly have known that Rilke would use one of these paintings in much the same way in his fifth elegy, written in 1922 as the center piece for the *Duino Elegies*, published the following year.

Wer aber *sind* sie, sag mir, die Fahrenden, diese ein wenig	But who *are* they, tell me, these travelers who are a little
Flüchtigern noch als wir selbst, die dringend von früh an	more fugitive even than we are, whom from their childhood
wringt ein *wem, wem* zu Liebe	wrings a—for *whose, whose* sake?—never
niemals zufriedener Wille? Sondern er wringt sie,	satisfied will? But it wrings them,
biegt sie, schlingt sie und schwingt sie,	bends them, flings them, and swings them,
wirft sie und fängt sie zurück; wie aus geölter,	throws them and catches them back; as from oiled,
glatterer Luft kommen sie nieder	smoother air they descend
auf dem verzehrten, von ihrem ewigen	on the worn carpet that has grown thin
Aufsprung dünneren Teppich, diesem verlorenen	from their eternal leaps, oh this lost
Teppich im Weltall.	carpet in the cosmos.

Rilke had begun his elegies in 1912, had gone through a long arid period, finally felt inspired again in 1922, and, having completed ten, wrote the one that begins with these lines and substituted it for the fifth, which was very weak. Picasso, on the other hand, turned out his paintings of acrobats one after another and had at this point completed more than three hundred paintings during the last six years, not to speak of his drawings. The choice he confronted was to repeat himself, doing much the same thing over and over, or to try something new again. Clearly, in his case the point was not to achieve some success through novelty. On the contrary, lesser artists keep working the mine that has yielded some gold, and only a very few of the most gifted, like Picasso and Goethe, refuse to stay with a formula that spells success and strike out in new directions.

In 1906 Picasso did some portraits that represent a sharp break with everything he had done so far, and "Les demoiselles d'Avignon," begun in 1906 and finished in 1907, revolutionized modern painting. Picasso had discovered Africa and what were at one time called "primitive" masks, and now he embarked on the course of destroying the conventional forms of European art. In a sense, what followed could be seen as a continual exploration of limits and a crossing of traditional boundaries. But it is more to the point to note that Picasso lost interest in *life* at the limits and that in his cubist epoch he turned his back on life.

Cubism did not require him to do this. Franz Marc, the great German expressionist, who was born one year before Picasso but was killed in action in 1916, carried over his concern with extreme situations into his version of cubism, but Picasso did not. Even when he occasionally returned to non-cubist representational painting, as he did, for example, in "Maternité" in 1921 and in "Mère et enfant" a few months later, not to speak of many other canvases whose titles are less suggestive of life at the limits, Picasso's concern was not with the edge, or even particularly humanistic.

Picasso's most famous painting is an exception: "Guernica." He did it in 1937 to protest the Fascist bombing of a small Basque town that was destroyed totally on April 26, 1937, by planes marked with swastikas that were executing this bombing mission for Franco. After it was hung in the Museum of Modern Art in New York, it became an object of veneration for countless people, a beacon of *art engagé*, and a humanist manifesto. It was possible to see the broken-up forms and the distorted faces of a bull, a horse, and of people as an outcry against inhumanity. Of course, the huge picture, three and a half meters high and almost eight meters long, was meant to be an indictment and was a descendant of Goya's "Disasters of War." But Picasso had employed the same means so often without any suggestion of an accusation that the outrage is communicated only by relatively melodramatic gestures—one Picassoesque head with two arms thrown up high toward the sky, and another lying on the ground with one arm extended over it, and a horse's head that is screaming, although the whole design of the head is anti-expressionist.

Perhaps one's reaction to "Guernica" is bound to be colored by one's initial experience of it. If this painting opened one's eyes to the brutality of fascism or the dangers of modern air war, one will always regard it with reverence. If one was aware of both and first saw the painting after World War II, one may be pardoned for admitting that it has always left one cold. That it does not transfigure terror, that it is not beautiful, that it is outrageously ugly, is no objection. Like Brecht, Picasso did not want to make the viewer feel elevated. He wished to show us the naked horror of air war against defenseless civilians. It may be doubted nevertheless that the style he had developed by this time and chose to use here was suitable. For all that, no other artist, including photographers, has succeeded in giving us any single picture that is clearly superior to "Guernica." However one chooses to fault him, Picasso remains a supreme artist.

35

Nobody would rank Käthe Kollwitz with Picasso. Her range was as limited as his was almost boundless. He was mainly a painter but also a graphic artist, a sculptor, and one who, to the end of his life, never tired of trying out new media. She was a graphic artist who refused not only to paint but to use any color, and the very few sculptures she did were a marginal part of her oeuvre. Above all, she confined herself to a single theme: life at the limits. And at no point did she *aim* to show that it could be seen as beautiful. Her many etchings, drawings, and lithographs of war, war widows, and orphans were meant to say what she actually wrote in bold letters on one of them: *Nie wieder Krieg!* Never again war!

It was as a social critic that Kollwitz showed hunger and misery and pregnant women going into the water. But she was a fine artist, and her work *is* very beautiful. It would be silly to add: in spite of herself. For its beauty does not impair her message. On the contrary, this alone makes it bearable to live with her etchings and lithographs, to keep looking at them again and again, and to absorb her feelings. The notion that ugliness and horror can be communicated only by horror and ugliness is akin to the notion that a novel or film must be boring to communicate boredom. Kollwitz did reach large numbers of people in Germany, though not enough; and the Nazis, of course, forbade her to go on working and did not allow her works to be shown.

While she never *intended* to show desolation, distress, and despair as beautiful, death was different. She dealt with it again and again till she died in 1945 in her late seventies. One of her works is called "Death Is Recognized as a Friend," and some later self-portraits, with the hand of Death on her shoulder, make one see how she welcomed death.

Several other twentieth-century artists have dealt with life at the limits more or less as Kollwitz did, but none has explored it so single-mindedly or with greater devotion and depth. Georges Rouault is known as a man whose paintings look rather like medieval stained-glass windows. Many people put reproductions of some of his pictures on their walls; but few seem to know his "Prostitute at Her Mirror" (1906) and similar paintings of that period, or his "Condemned Man" (1907), "The Tribunal," an attack on the courts painted about 1910, his "Prostitutes" (1910), "Fugitives" (1911), "The Widow" and "The Faubourg of Toil and Suffering" (1912), "Men of Justice" (1913), "Three Judges" (about 1924), or the painting of the hanged man that is inscribed *Homo homini lupus*, "Man Is Wolf to Man" (1948). Actually, many of his religious pictures fit into this sequence. His social conscience was central in much of his work; the wish to indict was clear; and the results were usually beautiful and haunting, not soothing.

What can be gleaned from Rouault's paintings cannot be missed in his graphic art. "Miserere et Guerre," a series of fifty-eight etchings begun during World War I and completed in 1927, has been called "a twentieth century successor to Callot's 'Miseries of War' and Goya's 'Disasters of War'" (by Shikes, page 246, who also offers reproductions of five of the plates); and some of his admirers feel that it is in this cycle that "Rouault has perhaps expressed himself most completely" (Courthion, page 296).

In the paintings and the graphic work of George Grosz social criticism is the constant theme, but instead of depicting life at the edge he became a cartoonist whose characters are savage caricatures of the rich and powerful. His art is descended from the well-known, influential lithographs of Daumier, but the Frenchman also did paintings of a very different nature that show a depth of feeling most unusual in the mid-nineteenth century. Daumier's lovely and poignant washerwoman with her little daughter, in the Louvre, is a case in point, and so are his various versions of Don Quixote, which influenced Picasso. He provides a link between Goya and Van Gogh, and in his lithographs he did supremely well what several more recent graphic artists have tried to do, too.

Few of our contemporaries have brought to our theme a distinctive sensibility; of even fewer could it be said that their whole work rings variations on life at the limits. Jacob Landau has dealt with it in virtually all his prints and paintings. Sometimes his titles call attention to our theme, as in "Vision of Dry Bones," "The Imprisoned," "Sisyphus," "Hunger," "Private Hell," "Bury the Dead"; more often they do not. His illustrations for *Out of the Whirlwind: A Reader of Holocaust Literature* naturally deal with the terrors of our time, but so does his "Fun House" cycle; and his huge lithograph of Dmitri Mitropoulos is a case in point no less than his print of Prometheus crucified upside down.

36

In the mid-nineteenth century, very soon after its birth, photography became an art. A hundred years later Max Wertheimer, one of the founders of Gestalt psychology, still told his classes at The New School in New York that paintings differed from photographs by being art, and many people still thought of photographs as mere snapshots. It was often said that the arrival of photography had led painters to forsake the imitation of nature, but since World War II a number of writers have shown at some length, with copious illustrations, how many major painters, including Delacroix and Courbet, Cézanne and Degas, Gauguin and Picasso have made use of photographs. The juxtaposition of some of the photographs Cézanne used with the paintings he derived from them (see Coke, *The Painter and the Photograph*) helps us to appreciate his artistry. Here we have nothing more than indifferent snapshots, and the comparison brings into bold relief the triumph of his style. With some other painters, however, it is not always immediately apparent from black-and-white reproductions which is the photograph, which the painting, and occasionally it is the photograph that is the greater work of art.

One of Etienne Carjat's portraits of Baudelaire invites comparison with Frans Hals' painting of Descartes in the Louvre: you can see the genius of a great man long deceased. Having lived with his writings for a long time, you suddenly come face to face with their creator and find yourself all but looking into his soul. Comparisons of this picture of Baudelaire with several other photographs of the poet and with etchings, lithographs, drawings, oil paintings, a woodcut, and a bronze bust, all of them based on one or another of these photographs, deepen one's admiration for the Carjat portrait. (Coke reproduces fifteen portraits of Baudelaire on pages 45–47.) This photograph, like Baudelaire's poetry, contributes to our understanding of life at the limits.

At the very same time, also in the early 1860s, Mathew Brady, an American photographer, explored life at the limits during the Civil War. He is perhaps remembered best for his remarkable portraits of Lincoln. When one considers that some of these pictures were actually taken by photographers working for Brady, and how impressive some portraits of Lincoln by still others are—for example, J. F. P. von Schneidau's daguerrotype of 1858 (Coke, p. 32)—one may wonder whether Lincoln did not simply have one of the finest faces any human being ever had and how much credit, therefore, the photographers deserve. But these photographers saw what most of Lincoln's contemporaries, who considered the man singularly ugly, failed to see. And by sharing their vision with posterity they helped to create an image of Lincoln that goes better with his greatest speeches than the caricatures reproduced in the newspapers during his Presidency. No painting of the man comes even close to the best photographic portraits, and the Brady image on the broken plate shows us a wartime President with such a deep sense of life at the limits that all subsequent wartime Presidents seem shallow by comparison.

On July 21, 1862, a *New York Times* report stated that "artists have accompanied the army in nearly all its marches, planting their sun batteries by the side of our General's more deathful ones, and 'taking' towns and cities. . . . The result is a series of pictures christened 'Incidents of the War' . . ." When Brady showed pictures of the dead after the battle of Antietam in his New York gallery, the *Times* said on October 20, 1862:

> Mr. Brady has done something to bring home to us the terrible reality and earnestness of war. If he has not brought bodies and laid them on our dooryards and along the streets, he has done something very like it. . . . It seems somewhat singular that the same sun that looked down on the faces of the slain blistering them, blotting out from the bodies all semblance of humanity, and hastening corruption, should have thus caught their features upon canvas, and given them perpetuity for ever.*

Since then life at the limits has become one of the staples of photography. One despairs of enumerating relevant pictures, but before World War II there were not many books that offered photographic explorations of this theme. In *You Have Seen Their Faces* (1937) Margaret Bourke-White presented a series of photographs she had taken of poor people, black and white, in the American South, and Erskine Caldwell, who was her second husband, supplied a text. "The legends under the pictures are intended to express the authors' own conceptions of the sentiments of the individuals portrayed; they do not pretend to reproduce the actual sentiments of these persons." Shades of Goya and Daumier. But Bourke-White eschewed caricatures, and the tone of the pictures and captions was never strident. The photographs, all in black-and-white, are beautiful, and one can look at them again and again and live with them. Only the first time around is the title of the book wrong, for few outside the South had ever seen these faces, and few in the South had seen them as the artist saw them.

Along with many others, Bourke-White created a record of some of the horrors of World War II. But perhaps the book that did most to make very large numbers of people aware of the ability of photography to transcend journalism and create enduring images of human life was a cooperative effort on a grand scale: *The Family of Man* (1955), subtitled "The greatest photographic exhibition of all time—503 pictures from 68 countries—created by Edward Steichen for The Museum of Modern Art, New York." The pictures, all black-and-white, were arranged thematically to bring together comparable scenes from different parts of the world, and many of the photographs were not especially remarkable considered by themselves. Some of the images, however, are unforgettable, and the whole was greater than the parts. Naturally, by no means all of the pictures showed life at the limits, and this is also true of another fine cooperative effort, *The Concerned Photographer* 2, edited by Cornell Capa (1972). The photographs by eight men include a very few in color, but none of these deal with our theme.

News magazines have carried thousands of photographs of disaster, destitution, distress, desolation, and death, and occasionally these pictures are memorable. But the news media are generally interested in what is sensational, and they rarely explore a subject in depth, either verbally or visually.

In photography, as in other fields, the feeling is widespread that as long as the content is interesting the work does not stand on its own merits. Because the competition has become so keen, it is assumed by many that to be artistically interesting a work has to be different, and that originality calls for a gimmick. Yet no tricks are required for photography to add to our understanding of life at the limits.

Films bridge photography and theater. Much of what has been said about plays in the chapter on Western literature applies to films as well. Many of the best and most highly regarded have dealt with our theme, often dwarfing the carnage of *Hamlet* and *Lear*. The range is wide indeed, from the small cast and controlled understatement of *Bad Day at Black Rock* to *The Battle of Algiers*. Most films, of course, are execrable, and people who grew up in the 1920s and 1930s were often told that movies, unlike plays, were mere entertainment. But subsequent generations are well aware of the fact that since World War II far fewer enduring plays than enduring films have appeared. And for every person who knows these few plays there must be scores who know dozens of memorable films. What needs to be noted here can therefore be said in a single sentence. The men who are recognized as the greatest directors—Antonioni, Bergman, De Sica, Fellini, Kurosawa, Visconti, to name but a few—are specialists in extreme situations.

---

* Quoted in *The New Encyclopaedia Britannica*, 15th ed., 14, 313f.

V

INDIA VERSUS THE WEST

37

Extreme situations are the staple of religion. The Buddha set out to conquer old age, sickness, and death; and priests of all faiths have built their practices upon delivery and death, disaster and distress, dread and despair. Yet religions differ greatly in their attitudes toward these phenomena.

A comparative study of religions in this perspective could be fascinating. But it could hardly be brief. Indeed, generalizations about any religion that has a history of close to two thousand years, like Christianity, or much more than that, like Judaism, Hinduism, and Buddhism, are perilous. But confronted with the realities of some of the cities of India, one naturally asks oneself whether Hinduism has anything to do with them. One is also led to wonder how Indian art fits into the story told here.

Having dealt with religions in depth elsewhere, I feel that it would be excessively cautious to refrain from drawing some relevant conclusions in this chapter.

One of the most distinctive features of the Old Testament and of later Judaism down to the present is the central emphasis on fellow feeling for the poor and suffering, for the orphan, the widow, and the stranger. It is not only in the Book of Job that those who claim that all suffering is deserved are roundly rebuked. The ethic of the Old Testament stands staunchly opposed to the wisdom of Job's so-called friends. The people of Israel are supposed to know from their own experience in Egypt how it feels to be a slave, and they should be able to identify with the oppressed. This ethos was absorbed by the Jews and has remained an abiding characteristic not only of their religion but also of Jews who have given up their religion. In wholly disproportionate numbers Jews have gone into medicine, excelled in philanthropy, and fought for the downtrodden. Moreover, the modern notion of social justice is ultimately derived from the Old Testament.

In the New Testament we find no comparable concern with the social order. *This* whole world does not ultimately matter; it is about to pass away, and what is most needful is salvation. We are exhorted to be prudent and think of heaven and hell. Insofar as the ancient Jewish ethic still has a place in this new dispensation, it is suggested occasionally in the Gospels that those who practice it will be saved. But there are many more passages that say unequivocally: "Whoever believes and is baptized will be saved; but whoever does not believe will be damned." This coda of the Gospel according to Mark is the leitmotif of the Gospel according to John. Moral teachings occupy a more important place in Luke and Matthew than they do in the other two Gospels, but Luke and Matthew also stress hell a great deal more, and the idea that God tortures the mass of mankind in all eternity, and the total absence of any sense of moral outrage on the part of Jesus and his disciples in the face of this, undermine and replace the ancient Jewish ethic. In the Gospels Jesus and his disciples feel no pity for the damned who suffer in eternity, and Christians of a later age cited the sixteenth chapter of Luke to confirm their belief that the pleasures of the blessed consisted in part in their delight at beholding the torments of the damned.

Twentieth-century Christians may feel like exclaiming that this is un-Christian, but what they call Christian are liberal attitudes that developed in a secular environment and were embraced by large numbers of Christians only in the nineteenth and twentieth centuries. In terms of this unjustifiable modern usage, the Gospels and the early Christians, Saint Athanasius and Saint Augustine, the Crusaders and Inquisitors, Saint Thomas, Luther, and Calvin were all profoundly un-Christian, and there was perhaps no more than one great Christian before 1900 whose attitudes really were "Christian" according to this usage: Saint Francis. And a year after his death one of his friends and closest associates, who had assisted him in formulating the rule of his monastic order, was elected pope and, as Gregory IX, burned heretics in Rome and developed the Inquisitorial system. Soon the Franciscans vied with the Dominicans to serve as the bloodhounds of the Inquisition.

The Christian churches did not raise their voices against slavery or serfdom but practiced both down to the period of the Protestant Reformation, and Luther still defended both institutions with impassioned eloquence. Ernst Troeltsch's monumental work on "The Social Teachings of the Christian Churches and Groups" remains unsurpassed; nor can one quarrel with his amply supported view that "with the New Testament alone, no social teachings at all can be generated" (p. 254) and that those who wished to justify egalitarian and democratic ideals by appealing to Western religious notions always had to turn to the Old Testament (p. 411). In the seventeenth century this move was made again and again by leading writers, including, for example, John Milton and John Locke. A new ethos emerged in the West.

The turn to the Old Testament was not inspired solely by the need for proof texts that might justify opinions that were held quite independently. Nietzsche spoke not only for himself but also for Milton, Michelangelo, and many others when he remarked in *Beyond Good and Evil* that "In the Jewish 'Old Testament' . . . there are men, things, and speeches in so grand a style that Greek and Indian literature have nothing to compare with it. One stands with awe and reverence before these tremendous remnants of what man once was. . . . The taste for the Old Testament is a touchstone of 'greatness' and 'smallness.' "*

Hindu sculptors carved marvelous horses—by the hundreds; for example, in the so-called Hall of a Thousand Pillars in Srirangam. But there is no statue in Indian art remotely resembling the defiant individualism of Andrea del Verrocchio's bronze statue of Bartolommeo Colleoni on horseback. Contemplating that work in Venice, or even looking at pictures of it, one understands how the ethos that emerged in the Renaissance differs from that of the Middle Ages and how people with such an image of man would feel drawn to the Old Testament.

India never had a Michelangelo or a Verrocchio, nor has she experienced anything like the European Renaissance. She was never shaken by the voice of the Hebrew Bible, calling upon her millions to become a people of priests, a people of literate individuals. The sculptors and painters of India remain cloaked by medieval anonymity, and their subjects are either nameless or gods. There is no Colleoni among them, no Jeremiah, David, or Brutus, no Nefertiti or Akhenaton. Only the gods are conceded such dignity, or, in the early Middle Ages, before Buddhism all but disappeared in India, the Buddha. For that matter, the finest temples and sculptures in India belong to the period before 1300, and art has gone steeply downhill since that time. There was no Renaissance, no rebirth, no recovery of Greek and Hebrew antiquity that brought new life. Instead of the inflated self-esteem that rose in Europe as one kept discovering new worlds to conquer, one lost self-respect as one was subjugated by the Muslims and later by the British—people with lighter skin who looked down on the people of India.

It may be tempting to say that they lost their spirit or that their spirit was broken, but we have no way of knowing how much spirit they had before the Muslim invasions. The Indus Valley civilization that came to an end about 1550 B.C., well before the first Aryan invasion, survives in archaeological digs that have brought to light ancient cities and small bronze and stone sculptures. This civilization is generally thought to have been influenced by the Mesopotamians, and the people who sustained it in what is now Pakistan had the art of writing. But from 1550 B.C. until the time of the Buddhist emperor Ashoka, thirteen centuries later, we have no evidence of literacy or of sculpture, temples, or other buildings in India. In other words, in what is India today the past is a blank until after Alexander the Great, except for a remarkable religious literature that was handed down orally, and committed to writing only during the Hellenistic age. Indian art begins during the Hellenistic period. And the contempt for people whose skin was darker than one's own was introduced neither by the Muslims nor by the British but by the Aryans who invaded Pakistan and India more than three thousand years ago. They developed an elaborate caste system, and their word for caste, *varna*, means color.

It is in the Laws of Manu that the caste system is developed most fully in writing, and it is, in one word, pitiless. There is evidence that in ancient times the two highest castes, the priests or Brahmins and the warriors or Kshatriyas, did not agree about which was higher, but they were at one in their conviction that they were immeasurably superior to the third caste, the Vaishyas, while the Shudras, the dark-skinned slave caste, did not need to be treated humanely at all, and the outcastes were still worse. This system provided the social setting in which the teachings of

---

* Section 52. For similar passages see Kaufmann, *Nietzsche*, 4th ed. (1974), pp. 299–301.

the Upanishads took shape, and it was sanctified by the Bhagavadgita or Song of the Lord, which is the most popular and most beloved sacred scripture of India.

The Bhagavadgita is profound, but it is also pitiless. Not only are the warriors told that it is their duty to kill without compassion, but Krishna, the incarnate god or Lord whose instructions comprise the song, proclaims in Chapter XVI: "Full of selfishness, force, and arrogance, lust, and anger, these malicious people despise me as they dwell in their bodies and in those of others. These envious haters, the lowest of men, I hurl ever into devilish wombs, birth upon birth. Caught in devilish wombs, deluded birth upon birth, they never attain me and sink to the lowest state."

Compassion for the oppressed and downtrodden would be as ill-conceived as compassion for the damned is according to Saint Augustine and traditional Christian teaching, or indeed according to the sixteenth chapter of Luke and other passages in the Gospels. To many Western people the misery they see in India comes as a profound shock, but no more so than the attitude toward it of most upper-class Indians. Most Westerners try to rationalize that attitude by saying that perhaps this is the only way of coping with such an environment; one simply has to harden one's heart and refrain from compassion to survive. But a religion could, after all, refuse to accept such misery as inevitable.

In the eighth century B.C. Amos, Isaiah, and Micah, as well as some of the other Hebrew prophets, told their people that the Lord hated and despised their feasts and took no pleasure in their visits to his temple.

> When you come to appear before me,
> who requires of you this trampling of my courts?
> Bring no more vain offerings;
> incense is an abomination to me. . . .
> seek justice,
> abolish oppression;
> defend the orphan,
> plead for the widow.

Ancient India never heard a voice like that, but it did hear the Buddha's teaching of compassion, and the Buddha rejected not only the authority of the Vedas and other ancient teachings; he also repudiated the caste system. The Emperor Ashoka tried to translate the Buddha's teaching into social legislation, but the Bhagavadgita soon after pointed a different path. And *in hoc signo*, in the spirit of Krishna's instruction, Hinduism eventually triumphed in India. Insofar as Buddhism survived at all in the country of its birth, it was viewed merely as another Hindu sect, with the Buddha as one of many incarnations of Vishnu. The caste system survived his challenge, as it survived Gandhi's in our time.

38

What is distinctive in Calcutta and other large Indian cities is not merely that old age, sickness, and death are out in the open, in the streets, instead of being concealed from view, as they are in much of Europe and North America. No less striking is the triumphant ethos of Job's friends who maintained that all suffering is deserved. The destitute are held to merit their lot as the more fortunate deserve theirs, for the Lord is just.

In the sacred scriptures of India, as in the New Testament and the Koran, there is no voice like Job's that impugns divine justice; there is no rebellion against the priestly claim that misery is punishment. Much less does the Lord say either in India or in the New Testament, as he does in the Old Testament, that Job has said what is right while his friends have not.

It is widely considered a mark of spirituality both in the Indian scriptures and in the New Testament that this world is disparaged as of little account compared to what lies beyond it. But the doctrine that misery and slavery do not matter because "a bondslave can be a Christian and have Christian freedom just as a prisoner and a sick man can be Christians without being free," as Luther put it,* is moral dynamite. It explodes the basis for social reform and medical practice and research. Jews and Buddhists cultivated medicine, as Christians and Muslims did not. Throughout the Middle Ages the only major field open to Christian intellects was theology, and slavery persisted in Christian Europe.

Again, it is widely considered proof of India's spirituality that Hindu teachers have made much of meditation and the quest for one's own ultimate trans-phenomenal self. The Hebrew

---

* *Sämtliche Schriften*, ed. Walch, Halle 1740–53, vol. XVI, p. 85.

prophets would have seen this teaching in a very different light, and we really fail to understand its import if we close our eyes to its social context and results.

It has often been noted that only the British put an end to the ancient Indian custom of immolating widows on their husbands' funeral pyres. It has been noted more rarely that the treatment of widows in India since that time raises the question whether or not their lot has really been improved. It is high time to contrast the Hindu ethos with that of Moses and the prophets and to realize that the individual human being of flesh and blood is not seen in India as being made in God's image and not respected as a person, regardless of social status. Women being burned alive and men, women, and children starving to death in the streets raise no questions for Hindus about divine justice or love and bear little or no relation to a man's spiritual quest.

Until modern times most Christians felt much the same way about the torments of the damned. The main difference is that in India you can find the damned in the streets. You do not have to go to a cathedral to discover them in stone friezes. But in the European Middle Ages one did not have to go that far either, and Christians also burned people alive—not all widows, to be sure, but only witches and occasionally Jews and heretics, rarely only one at a time. It was considered a small matter, seeing that God burned so many forever and ever.

Visually, of course, any comparison of the sculptures in medieval cathedrals with the poor in the streets of Indian cities is extremely far-fetched. Nowhere in art do we find anything like the realities of the streets in India. Nor could sculpture possibly come close to them. Painting might, but probably the only major Western painter of whom one might even think in this context is Breugel, and his style is so meticulous, so neat and clean, so graphic and devoid of subtle shading, that it represents an altogether different world. Rembrandt's style was more attuned to these realities, but his paintings are almost always dominated by one or two individuals. His ethos was radically un-Indian; it was rooted in the Renaissance and, above all, in ancient Israel.

In India herself there was no Renaissance, as we have noted; no recovery of ancient Greece or Israel; no rebirth of art through the development of painting. Sculpture was exhausted, as it was in Europe after Michelangelo, and the only kind of painting that developed in the postmedieval age was miniature painting which was introduced from Persia by the Mogul emperors and remained a highly fastidious and aristocratic form of art, reserved for elegant and gallant subjects. Painting in the manner of Bosch or Bruegel, Rembrandt or Goya, Turner or Van Gogh did not develop in India, and what was there for all to see never found a home in art.

It may be objected that what we see in India today is very different from what earlier generations saw. In 1706 the population of Calcutta barely exceeded 10,000; forty years later, 100,000; and in 1822, 300,000. Actually, the 1961 census still gave the population of the city as less than three million, comprising roughly two and a half million Hindus and less than 300,000 Muslims, as well as 50,000 Christians and a few Jains, Sikhs, and Buddhists. According to the census of 1971, the total population of the city was barely more than 3.1 million. These figures do not seem devastating at all. They could be supplemented with other statistics, and before long they will be, but in the present context the point is not that the horrors of destitution are not to be found in Indian art. It is rather that the extraordinary realities of Indian life, including its enormous and distinctive beauty, have no place in Indian art, nor, of course, in Western art.

Would it be going too far to say that Indian art is essentially escapist? That it bears little relation to the life actually lived in India and transports us into a realm of fancy? Surely, nothing could be more obvious. This escapism is deeply rooted in religion. This world is devalued, and escape from its alleged unreality is what is sought. Not to be absorbed in the miseries of this world, closing one's eyes to its suffering, not heeding the voice of your brother's blood is made a virtue.

To many people in Europe and North America this portrait of Hinduism is bound to seem hideous. For the peculiar spirituality of India has been largely misunderstood in the West. But that is not to say that Hinduism lacks profundity. Its most profound and distinctive symbol is the dancing Shiva. At one time, Christians made too much of the Hindu "trinity" of Brahma, the creator; Vishnu, the preserver; and Shiva, the destroyer; for this trinity plays no very prominent part in Indian thought or religion. Shiva, on the other hand, and his worship are ubiquitous, and he is seen importantly though not solely as a destroyer. As the king of dancers, the Nataraja, he is usually represented in a circle of flames, with a cobra, a Naga, entwined around one of his four arms, which suggest superhuman power, and with one foot he tramples a dwarf. The great goddess who is sometimes simply called Devi, goddess, sometimes Kali or Durga, is also associated with destruction. In its pantheon, Hinduism has never shut its eyes to the cruelty of the world.

Without ever mentioning Shiva, Nietzsche, who called himself a disciple of Dionysus, had his "Zarathustra" say in the chapter "On Reading and Writing": "I would believe only in a god who could dance." In that context Nietzsche was attacking the spirit of gravity and solemnity while extolling "light feet." But in Nietzsche's first book, *The Birth of Tragedy*, there is a haunting remark that he makes twice and then calls attention to in the preface he added to the second edition: "existence and the world seem justified only as an aesthetic phenomenon."* In a Western setting this is a strange dictum that needs to be interpreted as a retort to Schopenhauer. But in the preface the immediately following sentence brings to mind Shiva—though I am not sure that it ever *has* brought to anyone's mind Shiva: "Indeed, the whole book knows only an artistic meaning and crypto-meaning behind all events—a 'god,' if you please, but certainly only an entirely reckless and amoral artist-god who wants to experience, whether he is building or destroying, in the good and in the bad, his own joy and glory—one who, creating worlds, frees himself from the *distress* of fullness and *overfullness*. . . ."

The whole language of "justification" with its roots in the problem of theodicy, or justifying God in the face of human suffering, seems tied to a theology that wants to defend the goodness of the one and only omnipotent deity. If one does not hold to that, the very idea of "justifying" the world makes no sense. But that seems to have been what Nietzsche meant: morally, the world is unjustifiable, hideous, and cruel; but looked at aesthetically, it requires no justification. Nowhere is this more striking than in the streets of India. What outrages our moral sense is nevertheless beautiful.

---

* Section 24. See also section 5 and Preface, section 5.

EPILOGUE:

PHOTOGRAPHS

39

Photography can falsify; it can be an art. Instead of showing what the inartistic see, it can communicate a distinctive vision.

That black-and-white photographs misrepresent common-sense reality is obvious, but color photographs may seem to show things as they are. Actually, even those who tried to do that could not possibly succeed in Calcutta and Benares, and in many other places. Without its sounds and smells and the quality of the air, the world is not the same. Looking at pictures in a comfortable chair in pleasantly quiet surroundings is an altogether different experience from walking through an Indian city street or, for that matter, standing in the equatorial heat and humidity of Bali. Poetry has been said rather dubiously to be emotion recollected in tranquillity, although in fact some poets probably experienced more emotion in writing their poems than they ever had in the situations with which they purported to deal. But photographs are typically contemplated in tranquillity in settings very different from those they portray.

A photographer might seek nevertheless to show what was there, to report and provide information. So might a painter. But neither of them needs to aim at that. They could have any number of other purposes. One of these could be to mislead others deliberately to get them to do, or not to do, something—or, in one word, propaganda. In this spirit one might concentrate on what is ugliest or most outrageous, or one might even pose pictures or present what looks different from what it is in fact.

Without any wish to mislead, photographers are bound to give a misleading picture simply by concentrating on what interests them and omitting ever so much else. Thus almost all pictures of Sanchi in India are misleading. Even those which show the great stupa and not merely one of its four gates, or only some of the best-known carvings on one or two of the gates, give the viewer no inkling of the fact that the great stupa is situated on a hill, and that the place breathes an air of unsurpassed peace. Here one might well find oneself at the edge of life and contemplate it in the Buddha's spirit. But no photograph that I have seen of Sanchi gives one any notion of all this. On the other hand, this is something for which no picture may be needed, and words may be better.

Sanchi

The noise level rises as one goes south
from Basel to Naples, Egypt, and India.

On the hill of Sanchi near the great stupa
from ruined monasteries and temples
one hears only the wind. The plains all around
stretch silently to the distant hills.

Now and then a foreigner climbs the hill
and stays for a while, awed and inaudible.

Indians come up in buses, outyell
each other and carry transistor radios
clamber all over the crumbling temples
stepping on sculptures, spurning the steps.

One contemplating a haunting Buddha
covered with lichen and moss is asked

as *he* may have been a million times
as he sought enlightenment under the Bo tree:
Good morning, sir, what is your name?
Hey, hey, where are you coming from?

Even large monkeys with huge tails like wheels
move with a dignified sense of the place.

The Hindus move fast and never stay.
Only four of them sit
quietly under the stupa
enjoying its shadow and playing cards.

Photographs can be illustrative. They can show, for example, people playing cards in the shadow of the great stupa, or someone carrying a transistor radio as he climbs around the ruins. (See the last two black-and-white pictures.) Where photographs are used in this way, the question scarcely arises how typical the scene might be. Similarly, one might catalogue extreme situations and then offer one illustration of deformity, one of disaster, destitution, distress, and so on; perhaps also, for good measure, one illustration each of dread, despair, and other reactions to such situations. In that way pictures can be used as handmaids of a text. Where that is done, the sort of critical questions that are appropriate are whether the photographs portray real life or posed scenes with actors, and whether they really suggest dread or despair, destitution or distress.

Suppose, however, that you are confronted with a cycle of color photographs that are offered on eighty pages without captions. But you are told that the first ten pictures and the last two were taken in Khajuraho and all the rest in Benares and Calcutta, those of Calcutta beginning with the photograph of a book stall. Khajuraho is a small village more than three hundred miles southeast of Delhi and about half that far west-southwest of Benares. Being in the middle of nowhere, the Hindu and Jain temples in this area escaped destruction by the Muslims, and their erotic carvings, done about 1000 A.D., are world famous. Benares is widely known as the holiest city in India. It is situated on the Ganges, the holiest river of India. People come from all over the country to bathe in the river and wash away their sins, and many stay on to die in Benares and be cremated in one of the burning ghats on the north bank of the Ganges, hoping that this will bring salvation from the wheel of rebirth. (The last eleven color pages with pictures of Benares show scenes along the river.) And Calcutta is not only renowned as India's largest city but also as the most dreadful. Nowhere are conditions supposed to be worse. Accordingly, most airlines agreed in the early 1970s to avoid flying tourists into Calcutta, and the preferred tourist route became Delhi, Agra (the site of the Taj Mahal), Khajuraho, Benares, Katmandu (in Nepal) —or the same in the opposite order. (Anyone in Agra who admitted to having come from Khajuraho or Benares was presumed to have started from Katmandu, and if he said he had not, he was assumed to be confused about the names of the cities he had visited.)

One way of approaching such pictures would be to say: I have been in Khajuraho and have seen the famous carvings, but I certainly did not see any village scenes like these. Or: I have seen many pictures of Khajuraho, but this does not seem to be the same place. No doubt, many people would react in much the same way to the pictures of Benares and Calcutta.

To this one might respond by recalling the wooden statue of Jesus that appears on the back cover of *Religions in Four Dimensions* and also, much larger but without color, on page 122 of that book. A German professor who lives and teaches in Braunschweig remembered only the twelfth-century crucifix in the Braunschweig cathedral. The crucifix is famous and reproduced in a number of books and on picture postcards; the wooden statue is not. Yet the cathedral is far from cluttered. Its simplicity and austerity are virtually Protestant, which makes the wooden sculpture doubly striking. Even so, *most people see only what one is supposed to see*. They are at least half blind.

Something is radically wrong with our education. Most highly educated people have very little visual aesthetic sense. The architecture on most American college campuses does not prove this point, but the failure of the overwhelming majority of professors and students to as much as notice the mediocrity of the buildings that surround them, not to speak of being bothered by it, shows what is at issue. That such tasteless eclecticism is blandly permitted is as revealing as the fact that so much human degradation is blandly permitted in India, and in both cases the price of survival in such surroundings is to cease to notice them, to close one's eyes to them.

Some professors, of course, are deeply interested in the visual arts. But they are apt to insist that buildings make powerful statements. They intellectualize art, feeling that this is needed to make art respectable. They look for world views in architecture and for truth in paintings. Yet the value of art to a human being might well be that it offers us alternative approaches, different experiences—that it opens our eyes.

It is, of course, interesting and thoroughly legitimate to ask a person who sees something that we had not seen to tell us about it. A picture may be one way of doing that. But suppose someone looks at a picture and fails to understand why you admire it. Surely, you need not respond either, "I can't tell you, just keep looking," or "Because it makes such and such a true statement." One might instead proceed more or less as we did in the chapter on art.

Suppose, then, that someone said: "I have been in Calcutta, and what I saw was horrible; I saw maimed and starving people; but these pictures falsify the realities by making it look beautiful." Would it do to respond: "Much of the greatest art is terror transfigured"?

It would be tempting to say nothing, in line with the old Latin adage: *O si tacuisses, philosophus mansisses!* Oh, if you had remained silent, you would have remained a philosopher! But to advance our understanding of life at the limits a few comments may help.

The color photographs of Benares may be contrasted with Mark Twain's reaction to Benares, which is not far different from the response of most Western visitors, including Westernized Indians, even today. In *Following the Equator* he described a fruit, the dorian, whose rind

was said to exude a stench of so atrocious a nature that when a dorian was in the room even the presence of a polecat was a refreshment. We found many who had eaten the dorian, and they all spoke of it with a sort of rapture. They said that if you could hold your nose until the fruit was in your mouth a sacred joy would suffuse you from head to foot that would make you oblivious to the smell of the rind, but that if your grip slipped and you caught the smell of the rind before the fruit was in your mouth, you would faint. . . .

Benares is older than history, older than tradition, older even than legend, and looks twice as old as all of them put together. . . . It is unspeakably sacred in Hindoo eyes, and is as unsanitary as it is sacred, and smells like the rind of the dorian. (p. 953f.)

Actually, "hardly one building in Benares dates before the time of Akbar (1556–1605), and few date beyond the second half of the eighteenth century."* The Islamic invaders destroyed all old buildings and, as Ernst Diez put it in *Die Kunst Indiens,* "The old Indian forms were joined by Islamic domes and turned into a conventional mongrel architecture equal in value to that in nineteenth century Europe."

Mark Twain   was overwhelmed by the unsanitary conditions in the city:

I will make out a little itinerary for the pilgrim. . . .

1. *Purification.* At sunrise you must go down to the Ganges and bathe, pray, and drink some of the water. This is for your general purification. . . .

4. *Fever.* At the Kedar Ghat you will find a long flight of stone steps leading down to the river. Half way down is a tank filled with sewage. Drink as much of it as you want. It is for fever. . . .

7. *Well of Long Life.* . . . you will find a shallow pool of stagnant sewage. It smells like the best limburger cheese, and is filthy with the washings of rotting lepers, but that is nothing, bathe in it . . .

My Itinerary lacks a detail. I must put it in. The truth is, that after the pilgrim has faithfully followed the requirements of the Itinerary through to the end and has secured his salvation . . . there is still an accident possible to him which can annul the whole thing. If he should ever cross to the other side of the Ganges and get caught out and die there he would at once come to life again in the form of an ass. Think of that, after all this trouble and expense. . . . The Hindoo has a childish and unreasoning aversion to being turned into an ass. It is hard to tell why. One could properly expect an ass to have an aversion to being turned into a Hindoo. One could understand that he could lose dignity by it; also self-respect, and nine-tenths of his intelligence. But the Hindoo changed into an ass wouldn't lose anything, unless you count his religion. And he would gain much—release from his slavery to two million gods and twenty million priests, fakeers, holy mendicants, and other sacred bacilli; he would escape the Hindoo hell; he would also escape the Hindoo heaven. These are advantages which a Hindoo ought to consider; then he would go over and die on the other side. (pp. 956–61)

From Mark Twain's incredible condescension many Westerners have gone to the opposite extreme of seeing India as the center of spirituality and the source of salvation for the "materialistic" West. Mark Twain's reaction is essentially similar to that of many Christian missionaries, though he abhorred them, and invites comparison with a passage quoted in the last part of this trilogy (section 47). It is interesting how many responses to India and Hinduism fall into one of these two types: horrified revulsion or star-struck admiration. Reactions to Khajuraho are similar: either the famous sculptures (see *What Is Man?,* one is reproduced in Part III) are deplored as shockingly obscene or they are celebrated as "erotic spirituality." The photographs shown here do not fit into either mould.

40

Hell has the reputation of having a foul smell, and some parts of it do. But some of the very same regions are full of unexpected beauty. Indeed, much of it is so beautiful that one may wonder whether it really is hell. How can eyes trained to find enchantment in the sculpted marble draperies of ancient Greece fail to be thrilled by the incredibly colorful saris worn by poor women in India? And who walks more regally than women who from childhood have carried loads on their heads? But is finding beauty in Calcutta like finding beauty in Auschwitz?

It is not, but the tensions suggested by such worries are of the essence of these photographs. Most of the people in these pictures do not look depressing because they are not depressed. They are destitute but do not respond to their condition in the stereotyped way that one might expect. It is widely supposed, even by philosophers, that the natural response to death is dread; to disaster and to destitution despair. But this is patently false, and this realization spells liberation. We are free to respond to what befalls us in any number of ways. Some people are depressed for no good reason; others would have ample reason to be depressed but are not. Some are afraid of trifles; others find genuine dangers exhilarating and face death with equanimity or even welcome it.

* Professor L. F. Rushbrook Williams, *A Handbook for Travellers in India, Pakistan, Burma and Ceylon* (1962 ed.), p. 71.

Of the twelve conditions listed in the Prologue the pictures show only about half. Of the twelve responses, perhaps even less than that. Mostly the color photographs show people who live in very difficult circumstances with great poise and dignity. That they should be able to bring beauty to lives like these is a triumph of humanity.

It does not follow that this triumph justifies their condition, any more than Solzhenitsyn's *Cancer Ward* or *The First Circle* justifies Stalin's crimes or proves that nothing needs to be done about cancer. But we should be clear about what life at the limits means. We can come up against the limits in many ways, we can respond to the limits in many ways, and one man's limits are not another's.

Riding a motorcycle at a hundred miles an hour may be exhilarating for one and hell for another. Standing alone on a rocky pinnacle, with a sheer drop and splendid views on all sides, may be heaven for one and hell for another. People in the West tend to associate extreme situations with solitude, and the existentialists have unthinkingly accepted this premise. In Western literature it is typically the solitary hero who confronts life at the limits. In the Old Testament it is Jacob who all alone wrestles with God and prevails, it is David who cries out in despair, and in the New Testament only Jesus' sufferings are taken seriously. Pontius Pilate crucified Jews by the thousands, but in the Gospels there are only three crosses, and the malefactor who says to Jesus, "Are you not the messiah? Save yourself and us!" is not deemed worthy of salvation, while the one who says, "Jesus, remember me when you come in your kingly power," is saved. In the Western tradition both heroism and compassion have been for the few. We think in terms of individuals and poignant moments, in terms of what stands out boldly, and we are at a loss to deal with crowds and duration. We cannot cope with the spectacle of masses of poor people living in very crowded conditions, always. We prefer to think of such overcrowding as the result of some great disaster, some unique event, preferably the greatest disaster of one kind or another that ever happened, an emergency that can be met quickly and decisively with heroic measures. Our ethos was shaped by the urgency of the Hebrew prophets. We feel that there is no time to lose. We wonder whether we might not be able to help this individual here and that one there, and then we despair because there are so many.

Most people in Europe and North America associate nude children, sleeping in the streets, and being crowded, with extreme distress. Hunger is hunger anywhere, but nudity and sleeping in the streets need not be experienced as misery when the weather is not inclement, and Indians feel very differently about crowding than do most people in the West. A Texan may feel that somebody is invading his sphere long before a New Yorker would feel the same way, Italians and Germans do not have the same conception of what constitutes a comfortable distance, and most Europeans and North Americans feel acutely uncomfortable when anyone places his head as close to theirs as Indians often do. That the sense of distance varies in the animal kingdom is obvious. It differs from one bird species to another; it is not the same among herd animals and loners, like the rhino; and the conditions in which bees and ants thrive would be intolerable for some beetles. We may like to think that all human beings are alike in this and in other respects, but this is a liberal superstition. Even as some people are acutely uncomfortable when they have gone without a smoke for several hours while others have very different habits and would be very uncomfortable if they did smoke, people also experience crowding very differently. Even in Western countries some people enjoy being in crowds as they wait for hours to see the pope appear on a balcony in the distance; some like to be part of a crowd waiting for a visiting dignitary or a parade to pass; some go to attend spectator sports and are not at all acutely distressed when they find themselves among tens of thousands of people who are shoving to get in or out. Others really cannot understand how anyone can venture voluntarily into such situations. Some like hiking alone; others love contact sports. Some have their most intense experiences when they are by themselves, others à deux, still others in groups.

It may still seem as if the crowding in Calcutta must be too much for anyone's comfort. According to *The New Encyclopaedia Britannica* (1974) the population density per square mile in Brooklyn, New York, was about 32,100 in 1970; in Manhattan well over 67,000; in "Tokyo proper" 40,207; and in Calcutta about 78,000. In none of these cities is the density the same everywhere. Some districts are always much more overcrowded than others. In Calcutta, for example, density varies from 127 persons per residential acre in one district to more than one thousand in some others. "In 20 wards of north Calcutta, density was 590 persons per acre in 1961," which comes to 377,600 per square mile. It needs to be added that "There are few multistoried flats in this area. People live mostly in single-, double-, or three-storied buildings."

Some, of course, do not live in buildings at all. According to a study made by the World Health Organization and summarized in *The New York Times*, October 9, 1975, page 2, "50,000 people live on sidewalks of Calcutta, not 250,000, the figure long cited by city officials." Most of them "have lived on the same spot for more than six years," and the average family includes about two children and two adults, which means fewer children than most Indian families have.

"Not all the pavement dwellers are down and outers. . . . Some go outside . . . because there are too many others living in the same dwelling or particularly . . . when it is too hot inside."

During the monsoon one fifth of the pavement dwellers seek temporary jobs in rural areas. Some hold jobs in the city, others beg. Some collect pieces of coal that they can wash and sell for fuel, others "earn about 15 cents a day collecting rags, glass or paper that they sell for recycling." The beggars consider certain areas especially good, "but a beggar doesn't go there until another beggar dies." Those who have leprosy and look worst tend to earn the most. For less than 15 cents a day—at a time when the rupee stood at about 11 cents—the homeless could "eat a starchy meal consisting of a chapati, or of a bread in the style of a pancake, soup, or a paste" made of meat and flour. Of course, by no means all beggars are pavement dwellers, any more than all pavement dwellers are beggars.

Such articles and statistics conjure up pictures very different from those in this book. It is arguable whether any of the photographs show beggars. But it would be simple-minded to suppose that either the information given here or the photographs must be rejected. A newspaper account or an official report about the burning of the Houses of Parliament in London would have given one an impression very different from Turner's paintings. But after Turner we see other scenes differently, too. Often an artist or a philosopher says more than, "Here is another way of seeing things." He suggests that something important had been overlooked, perhaps even that our accustomed views are defective.

Common sense may retort: "What you show us is not the whole truth either." To be sure, it is not. We communicate in a context. We take much for granted. And when one of us shows how some of our assumptions were false and calls attention to what we had failed to notice, it is beside the point to reply that what we are shown is not everything.

The children in these pictures are not joyless. We may wish that they had different lives to look forward to, and some people may feel outraged that these children are not fired by the same wish. Nor are most of the people in these photographs consumed by resentment, as some of the beggars seem to be who pester tourists.

These pictures do not say: "Hell is beautiful." They do not sing the praises of the damned. But they open our eyes to new perspectives and prompt reflections on hell and damnation, on literature, philosophy, and art. Talking about these pictures, one could place them in any number of settings. Not the least appropriate of these is life at the limits.

Most philosophers have simply ignored it. The existentialists who have dealt with extreme situations have focused on death, dread, and despair, giving us utterly inadequate conceptions of human existence. One can learn more about life at the limits from some great poets and novelists and from some pictures.

BIBLIOGRAPHY

The text shows that a comprehensive bibliography of works relevant to life at the limits would have to include much of world literature and world art, most major operas, most of the writings of the so-called existentialists, most of the sacred scriptures of the world, and scores of films as well. If one added the secondary literature on all this material, one would end up with a multi-volume bibliography that would not be very useful. But the text is meant, in part, to open up the subject and to give the reader some idea of at least some of the major names and works that are particularly relevant.

Of the poets discussed in this volume, only Rilke needs to be listed here to provide more guidance; of the philosophers a few more. The reason for listing many more art books is that so many readers used to consulting books think of art books as only for art historians or coffee tables, or at most as a pleasant diversion. They need no guidance to find a collection of Shelley's poems or Shakespeare's, but they have no idea how one might find the relevant works of Goya or Kollwitz. And even most art historians are such specialists that they might not know. In some cases there are a great many books to choose from, but these will do.

Aldred, Cyril. *Akhenaten and Nefertiti.* New York, The Viking Press, 1973. Illustrated profusely.

Bruegel, Pieter. The greatest collection of his paintings is to be found in the *Kunsthistorische Museum* in Vienna.
The Complete Paintings of Bruegel, Notes and catalogue by Piero Bianconi. New York, Abrams, copyright Rizzoli Editore, 1967. Includes 64 pages of color and 164 black-and-white illustrations. The many more luxurious editions include *Bruegel: The Paintings. Complete Edition*, by F. Grossmann. London, Phaidon Press, 1955; 2nd rev. ed., 1966.

Callot, Jacques. Hermann Nasse. *Jacques Callot.* Leipzig, Klinkhardt & Biermann, no date. Includes 98 illustrations.

Clemens, Samuel (Mark Twain). *Following the Equator* (1897) in *The Complete Travel Books of Mark Twain. The Later Works*, edited by Charles Neider. Garden City, N.Y., Doubleday, 1967.

Coke, Van Deren. *The Painter and the Photograph.* Albuquerque, University of New Mexico Press, 1964; revised and enlarged ed., 1972.

Diez, Ernst. *Die Kunst Indiens* (*Handbuch der Kunstwissenschaft. Ergänzungsbund*). Wild-Park Potsdam, Akademische Verlags-gesellschaft Athenaion, n.d.

Goldscheider, Ludwig. *Roman Portraits.* Photographs by J. Schneider-Lengyel. Phaidon. New York, Oxford University Press, no date.

Goya, Francisco. The greatest collection by far is that in the Prado in Madrid.
The Life and Complete Work of Francisco Goya with a catalogue raisonné of the paintings, drawings, and engravings by Pierre Gassier and Juliet Wilson, edited by François Lachenal, with 2148 illustrations including 48 hand-mounted color-plates. New York, Reynal, 1971. Original French edition 1970. A magnificent book, but far too few paintings are shown in color, and most of the black-and-white illustrations are too small for study.
Goya by Francisco Javier Sánchez Cantón. New York, Reynal, 1964. A very large, expensive, and rare book that has been produced beautifully and includes 137 tipped-in illustrations, 58 of them in color, plus 56 full page color plates of the 14 murals of *La Quinta del Sordo*. The large murals are reproduced on three- or four-page spreads that fold out, and 28 details are reproduced full size. "The absolute fidelity of the color reproductions was obtained by printing them one at a time, checking each color separately against the original paintings."
The Complete Etchings of Goya. With a Foreword by Aldous Huxley. New York, Crown Publishers, 1943. Full-page reproductions of all the etchings. "In addition to the Spanish and translated captions of the *Caprichos*, from the plates themselves, Goya's commentaries on the etchings are also given."
Francisco Goya: Drawings. The Complete Albums by Pierre Gassier. New York and Washington, Praeger, 1973. Original French edition, Fribourg, 1973. A fascinating work.
The Drawings of Goya. The Sketches, Studies and Individual Drawings by Pierre Gassier. New York, etc., Harper & Row, 1975.
Goya by Margherita Abbruzzese, translated from the Italian by Carolina Beamish. New York, Grosset & Dunlap, 1967. Contains "80 Full-Color Plates," including "The Spell" (36, 37), "The Madhouse (44–45), "3 May 1808" (66, 67), and several of the late "Black" paintings (70–77). Inexpensive, unpretentious, and eye-opening.
Goya by Keizō Kanki, Tokyo, Japan & Palo Alto, Calif. 1969, Kadansha, has some additional color plates of the "Black" paintings: #2 and 80–86.

Heidegger, Martin. For an interesting bibliography of his works and lectures, see William J. Richardson, S.J., *Heidegger*. The Hague, Nijhoff, 1963, pp. 663–88.

A much more comprehensive work: *Heidegger-Bibliographie* by Hans Martin Sass, Meisenheim am Glan, A. Hain, 1968 (181 pages), supplemented by the same author's *Materialien zur Heidegger Bibliographie, 1917–1972. Ibid.*, 1975 (225 pages).

A surprisingly comprehensive bibliography of his own writings and of secondary literature is also included in *Martin Heidegger in Selbstzeugnissen und Bilddokumenten* by Walter Biemel. Hamburg, Rowohlt, 1973, pp. 159–74.

"My Way to Phenomenology," quoted above, is included in Kaufmann, *Existentialism from Dostoevsky to Sartre*, enlarged edition.

Jaspers, Karl. For a comprehensive bibliography of his writings, see *The Philosophy of Karl Jaspers*, edited by Paul Arthur Schilpp. New York, Tudor, 1957, pp. 872–87.

Kaufmann, Walter. See page 2. The titles show which books are relevant to what topics. The following books are cited in the text:

Cain and Other Poems. Enlarged edition. New York, New American Library, 1975.

Existentialism from Dostoevsky to Sartre. Enlarged edition, *ibid.*, 1975.

Existentialism, Religion, and Death. Ibid., 1976.

From Shakespeare to Existentialism. Boston, Beacon Press, 1959; rev. ed., Garden City, N.Y., Doubleday, Anchor Books, 1960.

Man's Lot. Photographs and text. New York, Reader's Digest Press, 1978. Distributed by McGraw-Hill.

Religions in Four Dimension. Text and photographs. New York, Reader's Digest Press, 1976.

Time Is an Artist. Photographs and text. New York, Reader's Digest Press, 1978. Distributed by McGraw-Hill.

Twenty-Five German Poets: A Bilingual Collection. New York, W. W. Norton & Co., 1975.

What Is Man? Photographs and text. New York, Reader's Digest Press, 1978. Distributed by McGraw-Hill.

Kierkegaard, Søren. English translation of all his major works have been published by the Princeton University Press, which has also brought out many books about him.

Kollwitz, Käthe. *Käthe Kollwitz: Verzeichnis des graphischen Werkes* by August Klipstein. Bern, Klipstein & Co., 1955. Complete, beautifully illustrated catalogue of her etchings and lithographs.

The Drawings of Käthe Kollwitz. Edited by Dr. Werner Timm. New York, The Galerie St. Etienne and Crown Publishers, 1972. German text (also issued with German title page) with 1467 illustrations, 150 of them full-page. A superb book.

Kosinski, Jerzy. *The Painted Bird.* Boston, Houghton Mifflin, 1965.

Michelangelo needs to be discovered in Florence and Rome.

Michelangelo, 5 vols., by Charles de Tolnay. Princeton, Princeton University Press, 1943 ff., 2nd rev. ed., 2nd printing, with foreword, 1969–71. Profusely illustrated, but has no color plates.

The Complete Work of Michelangelo by Charles de Tolnay *et al.* New York, Reynal & Co., no date. Contains 1040 gravure illustrations and 32 color plates.

Nietzsche, Friedrich. See page 2 above. For a comprehensive bibliography of his writings and works about him, see Walter Kaufmann, *Nietzsche*. Princeton, Princeton University Press, 1950, 4th ed., 1974, pp. 483–510.

Noblecourt, Christiane Desroches. *Ancient Egypt.* Photographs by F. L. Kenett. Greenwich, Conn., New York Graphic Society, 1960. There are many books with more illustrations of Egyptian art, but Kenett's photographs are exceptionally good.

Picasso, Pablo. Except for "Guernica," all the paintings discussed in the text are reproduced in *Picasso: The Blue and Rose Periods. A Catalogue Raisonné of the Paintings, 1900–1906.* Pierre Daix and George Boudaille. Catalogue compiled with the collaboration of Jean Rosselet. Greenwich, Conn., New York Graphic Society, 1966. Original French edition, Neuchâtel, Switzerland, 1966. 61 color plates, 770 black-and-white illustrations.

Parrot, André. *Sumer: The Dawn of Art.* New York, Golden Press, 1961. Original French edition. Paris, Gallimard. Illustrated profusely.

Rembrandt. Excellent examples of his art can be found in many great cities, notably including Amsterdam, Berlin, The Hague, Leningrad, London, New York, Paris, Vienna, and Washington, D.C. There is no book with nearly enough good color plates.

Rembrandt: The Complete Edition of the Paintings by A. Bredius, revised by H. Gerson. London, Phaidon, 1935; 3rd rev. ed., 1969, has no color plates at all.

The Complete Paintings of Rembrandt. Notes and catalogue by Paolo Lecaldano. New York, Abrams, copyright by Rizzoli Editore 1969. Includes 64 pages of color and 782 black-and-white illustrations. The black-and-white pictures are mostly very small.

Rembrandts Sämtliche Radierungen in getreuen Nachbildungen. Edited by Hans W. Singer. 3 vols. (actually, portfolios). Munich, Holbein-Verlag, no date. Also in English as *Complete Etchings of Rembrandt.* 3 vols. New York, Wehye, 1914–20. *Rembrandt Etchings: Reproductions of the whole original etched work*, by Ludwig Münz. 2 vols. London, Phaidon, 1952.

The Drawings of Rembrandt by Otto Benesch. 6 vols. London, Phaidon, 1954–57; enlarged edition, 6 vols., *ibid.*, 1973.

Rembrandt: His Life, His Work, His Time, by Bob Haak. New York, Abrams, 1969. Translated from the Dutch, with 612 illustrations, including 109 color plates. Includes sumptuous reproductions of many drawings and etchings as well as paintings.

Rilke, Rainer Maria. *Sämtliche Werke.* 5 vols. Wiesbaden, Insel Verlag, 1955 ff. All but three of the poems cited in the text are included in *Twenty-Five German Poets: A Bilingual Collection*, edited, translated, and introduced by Walter Kaufmann. New York, W. W. Norton & Co., 1975. The translation of the three others first appeared in "Rilke: Nirvana or Creation" by Walter Kaufmann, in *The Times Literary Supplement*, London, December 5, 1975.

Rouault, Georges. Pierre Courthion, *Georges Rouault.* Includes a catalogue of works prepared with the collaboration of Isabelle Rouault. New York, Abrams, 1961. The catalogue includes 565 small black-and-white illustrations. The text is illustrated profusely with full-page black-and-white reproductions and 49 color plates.

Williams, L. F. Rushbrook. *A Handbook for Travellers in India, Pakistan, Burma and Ceylon.* 19th ed. London, John Murray, 1962.

Sartre, Jean-Paul. See Allen Belkind, *Jean-Paul Sartre: Sartre and Existentialism in English, a bibliographical guide.* Kent, Ohio, Kent State University Press, 1970, 234 pages.

Shikes, Ralph E. *The Indignant Eye: The Artist as Social Critic in Prints and Drawings from the Fifteenth Century to Picasso.* 1969. Boston, Beacon Press paperback, 1976.

Solzhenitsyn, Alexander. The Feuer translation used in the text is from Walter Kaufmann, "Solzhenitsyn and Autonomy" in *Solzhenitsyn: A Collection of Critical Essays*, edited by Kathryn Feuer. Englewood Cliffs, N.J., Prentice-Hall, 1976, p. 162.

Alexander Solzhenitsyn: An International Bibliography of Writings by and about Him. Compiled by Donald M. Fiene. Ann Arbor, Mich., Ardis, 1973, xix, 148 pages.

Thompson, Hunter S. *Hell's Angels.* New York, Ballantine Books, 1967.

Troeltsch, Ernst. *Die Soziallehren der christlichen Kirchen und Gruppen.* Tübingen, Mohr, 1912. Page references are to the original German edition. *The Social Teaching* (*sic*, singular instead of plural) *of the Christian Churches*, translated by O. Wyon. New York, Macmillan, 1931.

Turner, Joseph Mallord William. Most of his major works are in the Tate Gallery in London. Black-and-white reproductions can give no idea of his art. All of the pictures mentioned in the text can be found in *Turner: The life and work of the artist illustrated with 80 colour plates* by Giuseppe Gatt. London: Thames and Hudson, 1968. Original Italian edition, copyright Firenze, 1967.

Van Gogh, Vincent. See *The Works of Vincent Van Gogh. His Paintings and Drawings* by J.-B. de la Faille. New York: Reynal & Co., 1970. Copyright 1970 by Meulenhoff International, Amsterdam. Only 56 color plates, but more than 2000 black-and-white illustrations.

Wiesel, Élie. *Night.* Translated from the French by Stella Rodway. New York: Hill and Wang, 1960.

ACKNOWLEDGMENTS

New American Library has kindly granted me permission to reprint several poems from my Cain and Other Poems. *The following poems, however, have not appeared in print before:* "Life at the Limits," "Willows," "Magnolias," "Riot," "Van Gogh," *and* "Sanchi."

Thanks are also due to W. W. Norton for permission to quote a number of poems from my Twenty-five German Poets.

Finally, I am indebted to the Egyptian Museum in West Berlin for permission to reproduce Jürgen Liepe's black-and-white photograph of Queen Tiye. All of the other photographs in the present volume are the author's.